TABLE OF CONTENTS

January 01

February 14

March 28

April 42

May 56

June 70

July 84

August 98

September 112

October 126

November 140

December 154

DEDICATION

This book is dedicated to all of my daughters

Margaret, Cece, Avalon and Roxanne.

You delight me.

> "And Suddenly
> You Know
> It's Time to Start
> Something New
> And Trust the Magic
> Of Beginnings"
>
> —Meister Eckhart

JANUARY 1st

I AM A BELOVED CHILD OF THE UNIVERSE

New birth is part of the cycle of things. All things are born and grow into what they came here to be whether it is an acorn or a ten-foot tree.

JUST FOR TODAY I AM HAPPY AND FULL OF JOY

Every day and every minute belong to me to learn and grow over time. It is a Universal gift from the Divine.

I APPROVE OF MYSELF

JANUARY 2nd

I AM A BELOVED CHILD OF THE UNIVERSE

The new year brings fresh ideas and dreams. I can use my imagination to set goals and to accomplish great things.

JUST FOR TODAY I AM HAPPY AND FULL OF JOY

Everything changes in its own time. I can make plans and set goals and enjoy today because it is mine.

I APPROVE OF MYSELF

JANUARY 3rd

I AM A BELOVED CHILD OF THE UNIVERSE

I love to play and to learn. I can play with someone or on my own. Playing is fun and makes me happy inside. I like to play games, dress up, in the garden and on the slide.

JUST FOR TODAY I AM HAPPY AND FULL OF JOY

When it is time to play, I can think of many things to fill my day.

I APPROVE OF MYSELF

JANUARY 4th

I AM A BELOVED CHILD OF THE UNIVERSE

I enjoy hard work that makes me think and sometimes sweat. Both work and play are important when planning to fill my day. What I put into life is what I get.

JUST FOR TODAY I AM HAPPY AND FULL OF JOY

Each day is a chance to fulfill my dreams and a chance to see what happens when my goals are met.

I APPROVE OF MYSELF

JANUARY 5th

I AM A BELOVED CHILD OF THE UNIVERSE

I am a good dancer, singer, and artist. I will show everyone my talents and share them whenever I can. Sharing my gifts is a blessing to the world and shows others who I am.

JUST FOR TODAY I AM HAPPY AND FULL OF JOY

Each of us is born with talents and treasures.

I APPROVE OF MYSELF

JANUARY 6th

I AM A BELOVED CHILD OF THE UNIVERSE

Giving and getting are the same thing. When I give something to someone, I have good feelings inside my heart. I like to give by sharing, by caring, and by listening to others.

JUST FOR TODAY I AM HAPPY AND FULL OF JOY

To feel good inside my heart, giving a little of myself is where I start.

I APPROVE OF MYSELF

JANUARY 7th

I AM A BELOVED CHILD OF THE UNIVERSE

I belong to a loving community. I have lots of support from the people around me.

JUST FOR TODAY I AM HAPPY AND FULL OF JOY

I love each person that cares for me. I show this by my actions, my words and by living in harmony.

I APPROVE OF MYSELF

JANUARY 8th

I AM A BELOVED CHILD OF THE UNIVERSE

I can speak up, slow and clear. When I have an idea, I can share it. I can speak up by using my words for you to hear.

JUST FOR TODAY I AM HAPPY AND FULL OF JOY

I am the creator of ideas. I can write them down or say them out loud. My thoughts are important and make me proud.

I APPROVE OF MYSELF

JANUARY 9th

I AM A BELOVED CHILD OF THE UNIVERSE

Each day is a new beginning. It is a new year and another opportunity to fill my days with learning and growing.

JUST FOR TODAY I AM HAPPY AND FULL OF JOY

I love others. I care for those in need. I look inside, and I like what I see.

I APPROVE OF MYSELF

JANUARY 10th

I AM A BELOVED CHILD OF THE UNIVERSE

My mind is as clear as the sea. I can sit still and just think about how great life can be. My mind is clear.

JUST FOR TODAY I AM HAPPY AND FULL OF JOY

I can let go and move on. When someone has hurt me and then said they are sorry, I am able to forgive them. I am a forgiving person.

I APPROVE OF MYSELF

JANUARY 11th

I AM A BELOVED CHILD OF THE UNIVERSE

I am grateful for a brand-new day. I plan to use it wisely and both work and play.

JUST FOR TODAY I AM HAPPY AND FULL OF JOY

Each day is another chance to be me again. I like who I am, and I want to share myself with my friends and my family.

I APPROVE OF MYSELF

JANUARY 12th

I AM A BELOVED CHILD OF THE UNIVERSE

Each day I wake up with two things in mind: how to enjoy the day with all that life offers me and how to serve humankind.

JUST FOR TODAY I AM HAPPY AND FULL OF JOY

I can choose how to fill my time today. I will be both joyful and helpful.

I APPROVE OF MYSELF

JANUARY 13th

I AM A BELOVED CHILD OF THE UNIVERSE

I listen deep inside to my heart voice. It is listening to that voice that allows me to make the right choice.

JUST FOR TODAY I AM HAPPY AND FULL OF JOY

I wake up excited for what will unfold from day to night. All things are possible as I sparkle bright.

I APPROVE OF MYSELF

JANUARY 14th

I AM A BELOVED CHILD OF THE UNIVERSE

The light within me shines brightly out into the day. Each moment is a new opportunity to learn, love and play.

JUST FOR TODAY I AM HAPPY AND FULL OF JOY

Today is stretched out as a gift to enjoy. I use my time wisely to learn more and to help others when needed. I go forth confidently and unimpeded.

I APPROVE OF MYSELF

JANUARY 15th

I AM A BELOVED CHILD OF THE UNIVERSE

I embrace the new day. Whether it is a new day, or a new year, everything I love and loves me is all right here.

JUST FOR TODAY I AM HAPPY AND FULL OF JOY

I am up and ready to go. I am eager to start another day full of energy, strength, and enjoy the possibilities that will unfold.

I APPROVE OF MYSELF

JANUARY 16th

I AM A BELOVED CHILD OF THE UNIVERSE

Life is what I make it. I wake up and remember to say thank you for another beautiful day. I can plan my time with work and play.

JUST FOR TODAY I AM HAPPY AND FULL OF JOY

One more stretch and I get up to join the fray. The light shines through the window, and I know the world is waiting for my special touch to lead the way.

I APPROVE OF MYSELF

JANUARY 17th

I AM A BELOVED CHILD OF THE UNIVERSE

I take care of my plants, my pets, myself, and my space. I water my plants and make sure my pets are loved and safe.

JUST FOR TODAY I AM HAPPY AND FULL OF JOY

I take the time to care for others and myself. The Universe cares for me in the same way, gently and tenderly every day.

I APPROVE OF MYSELF

JANUARY 18th

I AM A BELOVED CHILD OF THE UNIVERSE

I have an adventurous Spirit. I do not always know how things will turn out, but I am willing to risk making new friends and running about.

JUST FOR TODAY I AM HAPPY AND FULL AND JOY

A compass inside guides and leads me, and it will always show me the way. A new year, a new day, and new adventures are coming to stay.

I APPROVE OF MYSELF

DAILY AFFIRMATIONS FOR CHILDREN

JANUARY 19th

I AM A BELOVED CHILD OF THE UNIVERSE

Questions are good. I ask a lot of questions, and I learn new things. If I have a question, I ask it.

JUST FOR TODAY I AM HAPPY AND FULL AND JOY

I speak, raise my hand, or sometimes shout. When I have a question, I use my words, as I must get it out.

I APPROVE OF MYSELF

JANUARY 20th

I AM A BELOVED CHILD OF THE UNIVERSE

I think clearly about how I want to spend this life of mine. My life is mine to build and unfold over time.

JUST FOR TODAY I AM HAPPY AND FULL AND JOY

I am a dreamer. I use my imagination to create ideas and visions to hold.

I APPROVE OF MYSELF

JANUARY 21st

I AM A BELOVED CHILD OF THE UNIVERSE

Today I am moving on to new things, new adventures, and new dreams. I am willing to open new doors, and to make new friends to share all that life brings.

JUST FOR TODAY I AM HAPPY AND FULL OF JOY

Living in the moment I live joyfully on the planet with all living beings.

I APPROVE OF MYSELF

JANUARY 22nd

I AM A BELOVED CHILD OF THE UNIVERSE

I am wise and have good judgment. I make good choices all day long. Today I will use good judgment and make thoughtful choices that promote abundance.

JUST FOR TODAY I AM HAPPY AND FULL OF JOY

Like the owl, I am smart. Good choices allow me to feel good in my heart and create a life of joy of which I take part.

I APPROVE OF MYSELF

JANUARY 23rd

I AM A BELOVED CHILD OF THE UNIVERSE

I am healthy. My body is strong, and I take good care of myself. I wash my hands before I eat. I exercise my body each day. I get plenty of sleep.

JUST FOR TODAY I AM HAPPY AND FULL OF JOY

Like a lion or a queen, I am healthy, strong, and serene.

I APPROVE OF MYSELF

JANUARY 24th

I AM A BELOVED CHILD OF THE UNIVERSE

I have personal power. I am like a brilliant red flower.

JUST FOR TODAY I AM HAPPY AND FULL OF JOY

I am powerful over my feelings, actions, and reactions. I do not have power over any other people or the things that they do or feel. But I am powerful over myself and whether to act or be still.

I APPROVE OF MYSELF

JANUARY 25th

I AM A BELOVED CHILD OF THE UNIVERSE

Making mistakes is okay. Life means that sometimes we make a mistake because we are always trying new things. When I make a mistake, I can get right back on track to flying like a bird with new wings.

JUST FOR TODAY I AM HAPPY AND FULL OF JOY

Taking the right path is sometimes hard to see, but when I look inside, I can use my heart voice to sort out the key.

I APPROVE OF MYSELF

JANUARY 26th

I AM A BELOVED CHILD OF THE UNIVERSE

Finding and making beauty in the world is key. I find beauty in nature and in people. I make beauty through art and kind actions toward you and towards me.

JUST FOR TODAY I AM HAPPY AND FULL OF JOY

Beauty is all around me. In the clouds, the grass, and the apple tree.

I APPROVE OF MYSELF

JANUARY 27th

I AM A BELOVED CHILD OF THE UNIVERSE

My heart smiles within me for everything that can be. I embrace the future and always see the possibility.

JUST FOR TODAY I AM HAPPY AND FULL OF JOY

Today I accept that the love and kindness deep within my heart can make a difference in this world. I can lift a person's heart, and I can help make a fresh start.

I APPROVE OF MYSELF

JANUARY 28th

I AM A BELOVED CHILD OF THE UNIVERSE

I am proud of the choices that I make. I feel happy about the things I choose to be and do. My choices are healthy for me and my family too.

JUST FOR TODAY I AM HAPPY AND FULL OF JOY

When I do what is right, my heart soars high like a kite.

I APPROVE OF MYSELF

JANUARY 29th

I AM A BELOVED CHILD OF THE UNIVERSE

I am truthful. When I am asked a question, I am truthful. Being truthful means telling others what is going on with me. I am as honest as I can be.

JUST FOR TODAY I AM HAPPY AND FULL OF JOY

Telling the truth is not always easy. But when I do, my life is both lovely and breezy.

I APPROVE OF MYSELF

JANUARY 30th

I AM A BELOVED CHILD OF THE UNIVERSE

I am a grateful person who knows what is right. The expectation of a new day fills me up, and I happily greet the morning light.

JUST FOR TODAY I AM HAPPY AND FULL OF JOY

Each day is a beginning and another new start. I am confident and strong. I have a purpose and I do my part.

I APPROVE OF MYSELF

JANUARY 31st

I AM A BELOVED CHILD OF THE UNIVERSE

I am a smart and kind person. Kindness is a special type of wisdom.

JUST FOR TODAY I AM HAPPY AND FULL OF JOY

I know that I am not always right. So, I easily listen to other's ideas and opinions to add to my thoughts and ideas. The more I learn the brighter my light.

I APPROVE OF MYSELF

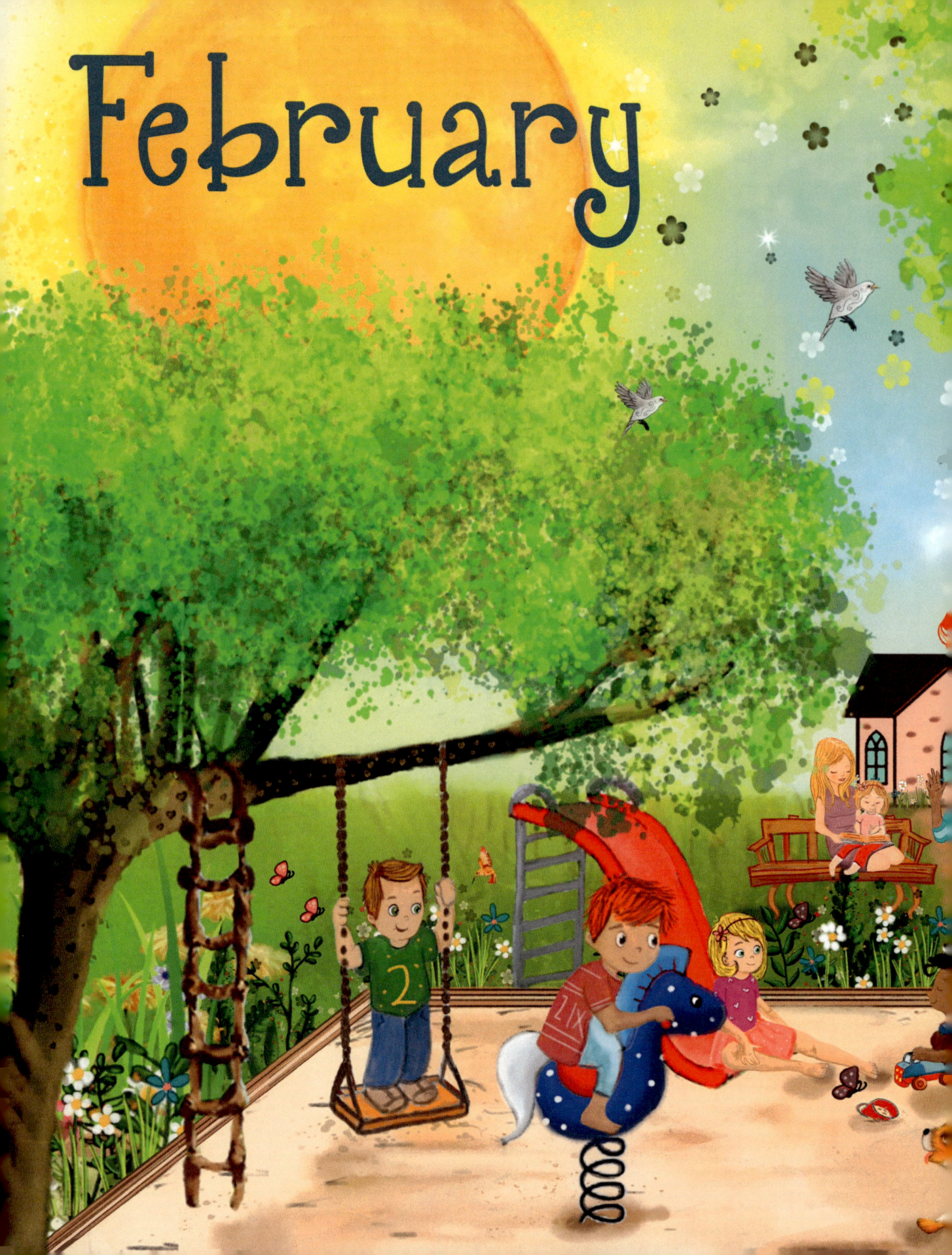

"When we put love out in the world it travels, and it can touch people and reach people in ways that we never expected."

—Laverne Cox

FEBRUARY 1st

I AM A BELOVED CHILD OF THE UNIVERSE

I trust my heart wisdom. My brains help me imagine and my heart helps me to feel the greatness coming my way. I use my head and my heart to create abundance each day.

JUST FOR TODAY I AM HAPPY AND FULL OF JOY

Today I listen to my heart voice as I learn at school and meet new people. I can access my own wisdom at any time, as my heart keeps me on track with its inner chime.

I APPROVE OF MYSELF

FEBRUARY 2nd

I AM A BELOVED CHILD OF THE UNIVERSE

I belong to the rhythm of life, and I can let go of the things when it is time. Plants bloom and then fall away, and classes may change with the sound of a bell. I can be sad about these natural changes, but I know that all will be well.

JUST FOR TODAY I AM HAPPY AND FULL OF JOY

Everything changes in its own time. Seasons come and go. I enjoy today because it is mine.

I APPROVE OF MYSELF

FEBRUARY 3rd

I AM A BELOVED CHILD OF THE UNIVERSE

All my relationships are joyful. I am joyful inside which helps me to live a joyful life and to create harmonious friendships. I am the maker of my own happiness.

JUST FOR TODAY I AM HAPPY AND FULL OF JOY

My life reflects my inner thoughts which are followed by my actions to create an abundant way.

I APPROVE OF MYSELF

FEBRUARY 4th

I AM A BELOVED CHILD OF THE UNIVERSE

I love my family and my friends. I can give love and appreciation to those around me. Showing others kindness is the key to living happily.

JUST FOR TODAY I AM HAPPY AND FULL OF JOY

I can show others kindness by lending a hand, offering to do chores, and by taking a cheerful stand.

I APPROVE OF MYSELF

FEBRUARY 5th

I AM A BELOVED CHILD OF THE UNIVERSE

I share my things with others. Sharing my things with another makes me feel happy inside my heart. I enjoy how sharing allows me to do my part.

JUST FOR TODAY I AM HAPPY AND FULL OF JOY

Sharing is a way to express love and kindness. My life is full of ways to make love visible.

I APPROVE OF MYSELF

FEBRUARY 6th

I AM A BELOVED CHILD OF THE UNIVERSE

Friends are a joyful part of life. I have many friends because I am a kind and gentle person. Friendship is a magical part of living. Friendships allow me to practice forgiving.

JUST FOR TODAY I AM HAPPY AND FULL OF JOY

When I am kind to my friends, the friendship never ends. Even if they move away, in my heart they will stay.

I APPROVE OF MYSELF

FEBRUARY 7th

I AM A BELOVED CHILD OF THE UNIVERSE

I cherish and honor those who take care of me and keep me safe. Our family members are special, whoever they may be. I love my family.

JUST FOR TODAY I AM HAPPY AND FULL OF JOY

My family does care, even when I am acting unfair or whine. They love me through thick and thin, and I tell them—when I am ready—that I am going to be just fine. I can start my day over at any time.

I APPROVE OF MYSELF

FEBRUARY 8th

I AM A BELOVED CHILD OF THE UNIVERSE

Some of us have brothers and sisters or uncles, aunts and grandparents who live with us. What makes it a home is the love and trust.

JUST FOR TODAY I AM HAPPY AND FULL OF JOY

I am a grateful family member, and sometimes I forget to say thank you, but today I am going to remember.

I APPROVE OF MYSELF

FEBRUARY 9th

I AM A BELOVED CHILD OF THE UNIVERSE

Each day is another chance to be me again. I love who I am, and I want to share my light with the world this day from beginning to end.

JUST FOR TODAY I AM HAPPY AND FULL OF JOY

I add joy and sunshine to this world, and so do you. I share who I am because that allows others around me to do the same too.

I APPROVE OF MYSELF

FEBRUARY 10th

I AM A BELOVED CHILD OF THE UNIVERSE

I am a good helper. I can help my family around the house and in the yard or wherever there is a need for a helping hand.

JUST FOR TODAY I AM HAPPY AND FULL OF JOY

If you need me, I will be there. I can help to water the garden or move a chair.

I APPROVE OF MYSELF

FEBRUARY 11th

I AM A BELOVED CHILD OF THE UNIVERSE

I do not waste things. I use paper wisely. I recycle items when possible. I turn off the water while brushing my teeth.

JUST FOR TODAY I AM HAPPY AND FULL OF JOY

Recycling makes the earth better, whether it is water, cans, or my old sweater.

I APPROVE OF MYSELF

FEBRUARY 12th

I AM A BELOVED CHILD OF THE UNIVERSE

I can care for others. When someone I know is sick, I can make them a card or bring them flowers. I care about how other people are feeling.

JUST FOR TODAY I AM HAPPY AND FULL OF JOY

When someone I know is ill, they can read my card when they take their pill.

I APPROVE OF MYSELF

FEBRUARY 13th

I AM A BELOVED CHILD OF THE UNIVERSE

Asking for help is good. When I cannot do something by myself, like tie my shoe or make a pot of tea, I ask for help. Asking for help brings others closer to me.

JUST FOR TODAY I AM HAPPY AND FULL OF JOY

Whether is it is for a drink of water or a swim in the sea, I can ask someone to help me.

I APPROVE OF MYSELF

FEBRUARY 14th

I AM A BELOVED CHILD OF THE UNIVERSE

I give from my heart a kind word, a smile, or a coin from my purse. We are all part of this family we call the Universe.

JUST FOR TODAY I AM HAPPY AND FULL OF JOY

Smiling is contagious. When I smile, others smile too. I do not have to do anything outrageous. Just being happy me is what I want the world to see.

I APPROVE OF MYSELF

FEBRUARY 15th

I AM A BELOVED CHILD OF THE UNIVERSE

Everyone is different. Some of us are tall, some small, some big and some have brown, black or blonde hair. It does not matter how you look; I am kind to all that I meet, and I am willing to share.

JUST FOR TODAY I AM HAPPY AND FULL OF JOY

Differences make the world a better place to be. The richness of life is made up of a beautiful human tapestry.

I APPROVE OF MYSELF

FEBRUARY 16th

I AM A BELOVED CHILD OF THE UNIVERSE

I like to explore. Learning and playing can be the same thing when I am exploring new places with my family or with my class. I am happiest when I am sharing a new experience with others reading a book, playing in a stream, or tumbling on the grass.

JUST FOR TODAY I AM HAPPY AND FULL OF JOY

Adventures are part of a rich and wonderful day. I look at learning as one of the greatest adventures that can be both work and play.

I APPROVE OF MYSELF

FEBRUARY 17th

I AM A BELOVED CHILD OF THE UNIVERSE

I am safe and loved. I trust that the people that I love are doing their very best, and when they fall short, I know that they can try again because life is a journey and not a test.

JUST FOR TODAY I AM HAPPY AND FULL OF JOY

I do what I say, and I say what I do in order to live in integrity. My words and actions are what people hear and what people see.

I APPROVE OF MYSELF

FEBRUARY 18th

I AM A BELOVED CHILD OF THE UNIVERSE

I am a valuable member of my family. The things that I say and do add to my family's happiness and well-being. My part in the family is valued.

JUST FOR TODAY I AM HAPPY AND FULL OF JOY

I am a flower in the bouquet called family. Together we make up a beautiful human tapestry.

I APPROVE OF MYSELF

FEBRUARY 19th

I AM A BELOVED CHILD OF THE UNIVERSE

When I am scared or unsure, I have courage. I can ask for help when something is hard for me to do or say. Courage means asking for help and facing what scares me anyway.

JUST FOR TODAY I AM HAPPY AND FULL OF JOY

If I fear the dark at night, I can ask for a special light.

I APPROVE OF MYSELF

FEBRUARY 20th

I AM A BELOVED CHILD OF THE UNIVERSE

I belong to you, and you belong to me; we are a happy family.

JUST FOR TODAY I AM HAPPY AND FULL OF JOY

The earth is full of many different families. Each family is unique. I am accepting and open to differences because it is differences that make the tapestry I seek.

I APPROVE OF MYSELF

FEBRUARY 21st

I AM A BELOVED CHILD OF THE UNIVERSE

I am fair. When I need to make a choice about who gets what, I am careful to be fair. I am fair when at home, at play and everywhere.

JUST FOR TODAY I AM HAPPY AND FULL OF JOY

Fairness is justice. When I am not fair, someone could be hurt. I seek fairness and kindness to bring forward and assert.

I APPROVE OF MYSELF

FEBRUARY 22nd

I AM A BELOVED CHILD OF THE UNIVERSE

I think about how others feel. When I see someone crying or looking sad, I wonder why they feel so bad. I can be kind to those who are struggling.

JUST FOR TODAY I AM HAPPY AND FULL OF JOY

When someone feels sad because they got left out, I can include them and then together we can all play and shout. It is easy to be a friend when I am out and about.

I APPROVE OF MYSELF

FEBRUARY 23rd

I AM A BELOVED CHILD OF THE UNIVERSE

I was born with a purpose for this life. Although the world is big, there is a special place in it just for me. We are One and each of us is full of possibility.

JUST FOR TODAY I AM HAPPY AND FULL OF JOY

I know that the Universe conspires to help me, I have everything I need to make my biggest dreams become reality.

I APPROVE OF MYSELF

FEBRUARY 24th

I AM A BELOVED CHILD OF THE UNIVERSE

I am part of a world that includes more than just me. I can reach out to others and give from my heart very easily.

JUST FOR TODAY I AM HAPPY AND FULL OF JOY

Being outside, playing, and kicking a soccer ball together is fun. Sharing in friendships is good for everyone.

I APPROVE OF MYSELF

FEBRUARY 25th

I AM A BELOVED CHILD OF THE UNIVERSE

Helping someone is love that you can see. I am helpful at home, at school, and whenever I can be. Helping another is my way of showing I care about my community.

JUST FOR TODAY I AM HAPPY AND FULL OF JOY

Whether it is with my pet, my family member, or my teacher, my helpful way will make their day.

I APPROVE OF MYSELF

FEBRUARY 26th

I AM A BELOVED CHILD OF THE UNIVERSE

I have the power to change my own actions or thoughts. Some things I am unable to change, like the weather, the day of the week, or other people's choices. I can accept the things I cannot change.

JUST FOR TODAY I AM HAPPY AND FULL OF JOY

When the sky is gray and it is a rainy day, I can still be joyful and choose to play. I oversee what I do and what I say.

I APPROVE OF MYSELF

FEBRUARY 27th

I AM A BELOVED CHILD OF THE UNIVERSE

I claim my privacy. There are many times when I need to be alone to take care of myself. I can shut the door when needed.

JUST FOR TODAY I AM HAPPY AND FULL OF JOY

Shutting the door is not unkind. In fact, it gives me peace of mind.

I APPROVE OF MYSELF

FEBRUARY 28th

I AM A BELOVED CHILD OF THE UNIVERSE

I can think for myself. I can listen to my inner voice and take the next right action. My feelings matter, and I can share them with others.

JUST FOR TODAY I AM HAPPY AND FULL OF JOY

I am gifted with bright ideas, like what kind of game to play to the shape of a cloud. When the time is right, I can share my ideas out loud.

I APPROVE OF MYSELF

FEBRUARY 29th

I AM A BELOVED CHILD OF THE UNIVERSE

I am a valuable member of my community. I was born into a community of love, and I am loved. I support others and they support me.

JUST FOR TODAY I AM HAPPY AND FULL OF JOY

I am worthy of being recognized by my neighborhood for being helpful and true. I also recognize others and all that they do.

I APPROVE OF MYSELF

"Behold my friends, the Spring is come; the earth has gladly received the embraces of the sun, and we shall soon see the results of their love."

–Sitting Bull

MARCH 1st

I AM A BELOVED CHILD OF THE UNIVERSE

Like a flower petal opening in the new season, my heart opens to love.

JUST FOR TODAY I AM HAPPY AND FULL OF JOY

Growing and changing is a new experience. I am ready to shine in all of life's brilliance.

I APPROVE OF MYSELF

MARCH 2nd

I AM A BELOVED CHILD OF THE UNIVERSE

I clean up my mistakes. Mistakes are going to happen, that is a fact. When I make a mistake, I correct it. I say I am sorry and then I change the way I act.

JUST FOR TODAY I AM HAPPY AND FULL OF JOY

Everyone makes mistakes because we are human. When I am wrong, I set it right. When I admit my mistakes, I sleep good at night.

I APPROVE OF MYSELF

MARCH 3rd

I AM A BELOVED CHILD OF THE UNIVERSE

I am excited about the springtime, and I feel joyful for change. My heart is filled with dreams of what today will bring.

JUST FOR TODAY I AM HAPPY AND FULL OF JOY

Flowers grow from tiny seeds, as does my Spirit, which sprouts with wonderment when I perform good deeds.

I APPROVE OF MYSELF

MARCH 4th

I AM A BELOVED CHILD OF THE UNIVERSE

I am healthy and make good choices. I take care of myself by following the rules. Rules are set up to keep me safe in the community and at home, like using crosswalks, waiting for the light to turn green and keeping my room clean.

JUST FOR TODAY I AM HAPPY AND FULL OF JOY

I am safe and sound when I follow the rules that are created to keep us all on solid ground.

I APPROVE OF MYSELF

MARCH 5th

I AM A BELOVED CHILD OF THE UNIVERSE.

I keep my word. What I say is what I do, and what I do is what I say. I do not make a promise unless I am going to keep it.

JUST FOR TODAY I AM HAPPY AND FULL OF JOY

I oversee my actions and my words. If I say I will feed my pet each day, I feed it before I start to play.

I APPROVE OF MYSELF

MARCH 6th

I AM A BELOVED CHILD OF THE UNIVERSE

Like a garden of roses with flowers so bright, my heart blooms with love and light. Living things grow and blossom when they are planted just right.

JUST FOR TODAY I AM HAPPY AND FULL OF JOY

I am the gardener of my own mind and heart. I am kind and honest which produces good things. Like the rose that blooms with so much care, I will bloom when I choose to share.

I APPROVE OF MYSELF

MARCH 7th

I AM A BLESSED CHILD OF THE UNIVERSE

My heart voice is clear if I listen, and it leads me to the right decision to make. Even when things are hard, I clearly see the right direction to take.

JUST FOR TODAY I AM HAPPY AND FULL OF JOY

I know I can accept any change that may come my way because I am as strong as a beating drum. I am as beautiful as the sound of piano keys, and I am as steady as the deep music from a guitar strum.

I APPROVE OF MYSELF

MARCH 8th

I AM A BELOVED CHILD OF THE UNIVERSE.

I tend to the earth by using my shovel to plant my seeds. The earth is alive and will nurture what I grow. I am the caretaker of my small patch of dirt. I know that I reap what I sow.

JUST FOR TODAY I AM HAPPY AND FULL OF JOY

I am the one to keep the earth fresh and green. If I do my part, we are all going to be happy and serene.

I APPROVE OF MYSELF

MARCH 9th

I AM A BELOVED CHILD OF THE UNIVERSE

There is a place deep inside my heart where love and kindness endlessly streams. My imagination allows me to move confidently toward my dreams.

JUST FOR TODAY I AM HAPPY AND FULL OF JOY

I am a successful person. I take the path that has been chosen by me guided by goodness and beauty.

I APPROVE OF MYSELF

MARCH 10th

I AM A BELOVED CHILD OF THE UNIVERSE

I have a plan today which I will follow. My family helps me stay on track so that I can be my best self as I change and grow.

JUST FOR TODAY I AM HAPPY AND FULL OF JOY

Planning is for winners. Following the plan is for both champions and beginners.

I APPROVE OF MYSELF

MARCH 11th

I AM A BELOVED CHILD OF THE UNIVERSE

I can adjust to the weather changing day by day. I enjoy the clouds, rain, and the sun. I wear the right clothing for the right temperature when I go out to school, work, or play.

JUST FOR TODAY I AM HAPPY AND FULL OF JOY

I oversee my health and my person. I strive to take care, so my health will never worsen. I practice healthy habits in every way to be a light for others every day.

I APPROVE OF MYSELF

MARCH 12th

I AM A BELOVED CHILD OF THE UNIVERSE

I know which way to go because when I listen, my heart voice tells me so.

JUST FOR TODAY I AM HAPPY AND FULL OF JOY

Pure love fills my Spirit and light radiates from my center being where I am steady. I always have everything I need to be ready.

I APPROVE OF MYSELF

MARCH 13th

I AM A BELOVED CHILD OF THE UNIVERSE

I was born with my own wisdom and healing powers. Everyone has different gifts. Some can sing, dance, or solve complex math problems. I have my own wisdom and talents.

JUST FOR TODAY I AM HAPPY AND FULL OF JOY

Today I will show who I am by being my best, which means using my skills to do well on a test or just being extra quiet while I rest.

I APPROVE OF MYSELF

MARCH 14th

I AM A BELOVED CHILD OF THE UNIVERSE

Springtime is full of new beginnings. The flowers are blooming, the birds are singing and with joy I am spinning.

JUST FOR TODAY I AM HAPPY AND FULL OF JOY

Springtime is a time when I pay special attention to all that is living.

I APPROVE OF MYSELF

MARCH 15th

I AM A BELOVED CHILD OF THE UNIVERSE

I accept change. Changing teachers, moving, friends going away, or getting a new brother or sister are all things that life brings my way. Change is hard sometimes, but I accept it because it helps me grow up more each day.

JUST FOR TODAY I AM HAPPY AND FULL OF JOY

Change happens over time for you and me. I accept change and adjust to what is rather than expect life to be, as I want it to be. I know when it comes to change, I can only change me.

I APPROVE OF MYSELF

MARCH 16th

I AM A BELOVED CHILD OF THE UNIVERSE

I am Spirit. I have a body, but I also have a Spirit. My Spirit helps me to know who I am, be my best self, and know that I am safe, whole, and loved.

JUST FOR TODAY I AM HAPPY AND FULL OF JOY

I am lots of things, but the one thing that is key is the fact that I am much more than what you see. I love me.

I APPROVE OF MYSELF

MARCH 17th

I AM A BELOVED CHILD OF THE UNIVERSE

I am flexible. When things do not go my way, I can adjust. I am not the only one who has things that they want and need. I am enough just being me.

JUST FOR TODAY I AM HAPPY AND FULL OF JOY

Each new day brings opportunities for my life to embrace. I have an endless well of grace.

I APPROVE OF MYSELF

MARCH 18th

I AM A BELOVED CHILD OF THE UNIVERSE

Everything has its own meaning and essence. Weather can be stormy or sunny. Land can be flat or have mountains with springs. I see the beauty in all these things.

JUST FOR TODAY I AM HAPPY AND FULL OF JOY

Raindrops fall and nurture the thirsty ground. I can see the beauty on a rainy day even if I cannot go out and play.

I APPROVE OF MYSELF

MARCH 19th

I AM A BELOVED CHILD OF THE UNIVERSE

I am creative. I see in my mind what it is that I want to draw, and I draw it. I can use my imagination to do lots of things. I can use it to draw, write, take pictures, and to sing.

JUST FOR TODAY I AM HAPPY AND FULL OF JOY

Whether it is creating games, art, poetry, or doing my school work, using my insight is the key to launching myself into flight.

I APPROVE OF MYSELF

MARCH 20th

I AM A BELOVED CHILD OF THE UNIVERSE

I can tackle new problems and new situations at school or at home. I embrace the unknown, understanding that I am never alone.

JUST FOR TODAY I AM HAPPY AND FULL OF JOY

When I am taking a new direction, meeting new people, or changing schools, I will know inside how to move along. Life is for the living and I live this day brave and strong.

I APPROVE OF MYSELF

MARCH 21st

I AM A BELOVED CHILD OF THE UNIVERSE

I am open-minded. I listen to others even when it is hard. Everyone has ideas and thinks that their ideas are best. I listen with an open mind so that I can learn from others and keep my heart at rest.

JUST FOR TODAY I AM HAPPY AND FULL OF JOY

An open mind is like a waterspout. It is constantly running over with a life source that I can wonder about. I am open-minded.

I APPROVE OF MYSELF

MARCH 22ⁿᵈ

I AM A BELOVED CHILD OF THE UNIVERSE

I celebrate change. Springtime is for wonder and play. I finish my studies, pick up my things, and go outside. I look forward to a bright and blooming spring day.

JUST FOR TODAY I AM HAPPY AND FULL OF JOY

I celebrate the changing seasons. For my joyfulness, there are many reasons.

I APPROVE OF MYSELF

MARCH 23ʳᵈ

I AM A BELOVED CHILD OF THE UNIVERSE

I was born with love bursting out of me from inside. Love is the magic that heals all things. When someone is not feeling well, I can sit with them and fill them up with the energy that kindness brings.

JUST FOR TODAY I AM HAPPY AND FULL OF JOY

I am love. I do not have to try to love because I am love. I just must be me for all the world to see.

I APPROVE OF MYSELF

MARCH 24ᵗʰ

I AM A BELOVED CHILD OF THE UNIVERSE

I was created with an inner light. That light shines all the time. I use that light to light the way for others and to clearly see the path that is mine.

JUST FOR TODAY I AM HAPPY AND FULL OF JOY

This light of mine was in me at birth, and it will be with me as I grow. I am safe and protected, this I do know.

I APPROVE OF MYSELF

MARCH 25th

I AM A BELOVED CHILD OF THE UNIVERSE

I can start over at any time. First thing in the morning, the afternoon or even at night, when I need to start again, it is alright.

JUST FOR TODAY I AM HAPPY AND FULL OF JOY

If I need to restart in the middle of the day, that choice can help me begin a positive shift. My mind is open to reflecting and forgiving, and that is a gift.

I APPROVE OF MYSELF

MARCH 26th

I AM A BELOVED CHILD OF THE UNIVERSE

I choose my thoughts. No one can control what I think. I learn at school, at home, and on the screen. However, only I control my thoughts. I choose what I believe and what I do not.

JUST FOR TODAY I AM HAPPY AND FULL OF JOY

The greatest gift I have is my brain. I realize that my brain is my superpower that allows me to have an imagination. My imagination is my true strength. To guard my brain, I will go to any length.

I APPROVE OF MYSELF

MARCH 27th

I AM A BELOVED CHILD OF THE UNIVERSE

I am exactly how I am supposed to be. I am a loving creature put on this planet to create. I can draw, dance, learn, teach, build, and sing. I am a creator of many things.

JUST FOR TODAY I AM HAPPY AND FULL OF JOY

I am here to create beauty and truth. I belong to the universe, which means that I have a responsibility to make the world a better place. I am valuable and know that I am connected to everyone in the human race.

I APPROVE OF MYSELF

MARCH 28th

I AM A BELOVED CHILD OF THE UNIVERSE

What I think matters. I create my environment with my thoughts. If I think I am brilliant, talented, and valuable, I am and so are you. No one can take away my thoughts. I am what I think I am, and you are too.

JUST FOR TODAY I AM HAPPY AND FULL OF JOY

Each of us belongs to the other. When I am responsible for what I think, it gives me a chance to be of service. Together we build a community that allows for a sense of unity.

I APPROVE OF MYSELF

MARCH 29th

I AM A BELOVED CHILD OF THE UNIVERSE

Life is full of change. Each year my teachers change, the seasons change, and I get taller and learn different things. I live open to change and embrace all that life brings.

JUST FOR TODAY I AM HAPPY AND FULL OF JOY

Change is something I look forward to. I stay the same inside and the people that love me are forever in my life even after they move on and must go. I embrace change to improve myself and to grow.

I APPROVE OF MYSELF

MARCH 30th

I AM A BELOVED CHILD OF THE UNIVERSE

I have plenty of time to do what needs to be done today. I do not need to feel rushed or hurried. Life flows like water, and I am along for the joyful ride without stress or worry.

JUST FOR TODAY I AM HAPPY AND FULL OF JOY

I have all the time that I need to do what needs to be done. I never need to feel like I am too slow or that I have not done enough on any given day. I am here to work and to play.

I APPROVE OF MYSELF

MARCH 31ˢᵗ

I AM A BELOVED CHILD OF THE UNIVERSE

Springtime is here, and all around me is new life today. I see new blossoms and flowers, and when I go outside, I want to dance and play.

JUST FOR TODAY I AM HAPPY AND FULL OF JOY

Sweet blessings of spring are plentiful and free. I like the smell of the air, playing and drawing outside, and seeing a butterfly circling around the flowers with a bee.

I APPROVE OF MYSELF

"Never Allow Waiting
To Become a Habit.
Live in Your Dreams
And Take Risks.
Life is Happening Now."

—Paulo Coelho

APRIL 1st

I AM A BELOVED CHILD OF THE UNIVERSE

When I feel good, the world is a good place and good things come my way. I focus my powerful mind on good thoughts and choose carefully how to spend my day.

JUST FOR TODAY I AM HAPPY AND FULL OF JOY

Life is full of ups and downs. I focus on the ups, and I rather not join those who frown. I make my own luck, and I cheer on the team with my powerful strong mind that can achieve any dream.

I APPROVE OF MYSELF

APRIL 2nd

I AM A BELOVED CHILD OF THE UNIVERSE

To create is to make something that no one else has made. I am a creator. I can draw, dance, think, imagine, and play music. I do not need anyone's approval when I am being creative.

JUST FOR TODAY I AM HAPPY AND FULL OF JOY

My imagination is a gift that I can use every day. There are so many ways for me to express my ideas. I can express my ideas through both my work and through my play.

I APPROVE OF MYSELF

APRIL 3rd

I AM A BELOVED CHILD OF THE UNIVERSE

I was born a gift to this world and my family, just like the birds, the flowers, and the bumblebee.

JUST FOR TODAY I AM HAPPY AND FULL OF JOY

My heart is full of joy as the seasons change and new life unfolds. I am filled with new ideas, and I practice kind acts for both the young and old.

I APPROVE OF MYSELF

APRIL 4th

I AM A BELOVED CHILD OF THE UNIVERSE

I care about how animals feel. If an animal is sick or hurt, I tell an adult to see if we can help the animal heal.

JUST FOR TODAY I AM HAPPY AND FULL OF JOY

If my pet is sick or feeling scared, I can hold it near, so it knows that I care and that I love it dear.

I APPROVE OF MYSELF

APRIL 5th

I AM A BELOVED CHILD OF THE UNIVERSE

I am full of new beginnings today. I have another opportunity to make new friends and to learn new things at work and play.

JUST FOR TODAY I AM HAPPY AND FULL OF JOY

I love to learn. I am never too old or young to learn something new or to make a new friend. Life has given me the magic of learning and being, from beginning to end.

I APPROVE OF MYSELF

APRIL 6th

I AM A BELOVED CHILD OF THE UNIVERSE

I am part of something much bigger than me and much of it I cannot see.

JUST FOR TODAY I AM HAPPY AND FULL OF JOY

The Creator of all things is in me and in you. We live our lives in a way that benefits one another and the earth. Our planet is the true Mother.

I APPROVE OF MYSELF

APRIL 7th

I AM A BELOVED CHILD OF THE UNIVERSE

I am the maker of my own luck. I see what I need to get things done and then my task is almost won. I follow through on what I say I will do.

JUST FOR TODAY I AM HAPPY AND FULL OF JOY

I am the creator of my own good fortune. It might be to get a good grade, or it may be to join a parade.

I APPROVE OF MYSELF

APRIL 8th

I AM A BELOVED CHILD OF THE UNIVERSE

Imagination is the key to creating my own art. I sit and focus and see my masterpiece from the start.

JUST FOR TODAY I AM HAPPY AND FULL OF JOY

In my mind, I have unlimited power to create. I think of the thing I want to create and then it is given to me as fate.

I APPROVE OF MYSELF

APRIL 9th

I AM A BELOVED CHILD OF THE UNIVERSE

My body is strong, and it can heal on its own. My mind and body are perfectly orchestrated to mend every cell and heal every bone.

JUST FOR TODAY I AM HAPPY AND FULL OF JOY

I am a healer of both myself and those around me. We are each born with all the tools we need to heal and to be healed.

I APPROVE OF MYSELF

APRIL 10th

I AM A BELOVED CHILD OF THE UNIVERSE

I do what I say, and I say what I do. I keep my word.

JUST FOR TODAY I AM HAPPY AND FULL OF JOY

When I keep my word, the people around me can depend on me to follow through. Following through makes this a healthy relationship for me and for you.

I APPROVE OF MYSELF

APRIL 11th

I AM A BELOVED CHILD OF THE UNIVERSE

I belong to my family. Every family is different. Sometimes there is a mom and a dad or a grandparent or an aunt that takes care of the kids and who will give them a voice. Sometimes it is a kind person who chose to raise a child and become their family by choice.

JUST FOR TODAY I AM HAPPY AND FULL OF JOY

Every family is different, like a beautiful song. The important thing to remember is that it is to each other, that we belong.

I APPROVE OF MYSELF

APRIL 12th

I AM A BELOVED CHILD OF THE UNIVERSE

I am part of Nature's plans. Nature's grace brings forth new flowers and plants sprouting from roots deep within the earth. I too come from the miracle of birth.

JUST FOR TODAY I AM HAPPY AND FULL OF JOY

Nature's kindness paves the way for joy, wonder, beauty, and happiness without expectation. Her grace is free and available to you and to me.

I APPROVE OF MYSELF

APRIL 13th

I AM A BELOVED CHILD OF THE UNIVERSE

Life is more than what I can see. Love, hope, and faith are invisible to me. But I can feel each of these gifts which I am given for free.

JUST FOR TODAY I AM HAPPY AND FULL OF JOY

The best things in life are things I cannot see. The best things in life are love, faith, and hope, which are given to me abundantly.

I APPROVE OF MYSELF

APRIL 14th

I AM A BELOVED CHILD OF THE UNIVERSE

I care for myself by sitting still each day before I go out to start my work or my play. Listening to my heart voice is important to me so that when I am with you, I can share and just be.

JUST FOR TODAY I AM HAPPY AND FULL OF JOY

When I am centered in myself, I am at my best. I can then see clearly how to serve my community or take a test.

I APPROVE OF MYSELF

APRIL 15th

I AM A BELOVED CHILD OF THE UNIVERSE

Nature is all around me whether I am in the country or in the city. I find comfort in nature because I am connected with all living things.

JUST FOR TODAY I AM HAPPY AND FULL OF JOY

Whether it is a bug, a bird, a slug, or a bee, all things are connected, so I must cherish each creature that I happen to see.

I APPROVE OF MYSELF

APRIL 16th

I AM A BELOVED CHILD OF THE UNIVERSE

I like to learn because learning is fun. Whether it be at school or from my family at home, I can learn because my mind is like a sponge.

JUST FOR TODAY I AM HAPPY AND FULL OF JOY

I am smart, and I am always willing to learn with my open mind and my open heart.

I APPROVE OF MYSELF

APRIL 17th

I AM A BELOVED CHILD OF THE UNIVERSE

The world is huge. I am but a part of an entire universe of clouds, dirt, water, and energy. I am made of everything including the sky, earth, stars, and the Universal memory.

JUST FOR TODAY I AM HAPPY AND FULL OF JOY

I am here to love and serve, and I have everything I need to help myself and others succeed.

I APPROVE OF MYSELF

APRIL 18th

I AM A BELOVED CHILD OF THE UNIVERSE

Love is healing medicine for all that needs to get better. I can extend my heart to help, and we can solve the problem together.

JUST FOR TODAY I AM HAPPY AND FULL OF JOY

Just being peaceful, open, and joyful can help the planet heal. Although it is something we cannot see, love can heal because love is real.

I APPROVE OF MYSELF

APRIL 19th

I AM A BELOVED CHILD OF THE UNIVERSE

I give praise freely. I see when others are trying their best. I make sure to be kind and cheer them on with the rest.

JUST FOR TODAY I AM HAPPY AND FULL OF JOY

When others succeed, it makes me smile. Life is for cooperation, not competition. I am better when we all succeed and when we all go that extra mile.

I APPROVE OF MYSELF

APRIL 20th

I AM A BELOVED CHILD OF THE UNIVERSE

My heart voice is guided by the Universal truths inside of me from birth. I was born strong and kind, and to value each of our inherent worth.

JUST FOR TODAY I AM HAPPY AND FULL OF JOY

I have a code for myself of how I want to be, this code will lead me to be happy, joyous, and free.

I APPROVE OF MYSELF

APRIL 21st

I AM A BELOVED CHILD OF THE UNIVERSE

I see possibilities and opportunities everywhere. I focus on what I have now this minute. In this mindset, there is no despair.

JUST FOR TODAY I AM HAPPY AND FULL OF JOY

I am a positive thinker. I see the glass half full when others do not. I believe that we can make any situation better with a positive thought.

I APPROVE OF MYSELF

APRIL 22nd

I AM A BELOVED CHILD OF THE UNIVERSE

I am here for those I love. Through thick and thin I stick to their side because my family and friends are who I walk alongside.

JUST FOR TODAY I AM HAPPY AND FULL OF JOY

Loyalty is important to remember and helps to build trust. We are here for our families, and they are here for us.

I APPROVE OF MYSELF

APRIL 23rd

I AM A BELOVED CHILD OF THE UNIVERSE

I cherish new life. Spring is full of new life. One day the seed is under the ground, and the next day the plant pops up and a flower bursts forth, bright and round.

JUST FOR TODAY I AM HAPPY AND FULL OF JOY

I can join nature's orchestra of a colorful garden song. I play my part as the planter, pull up some weeds, water the soil, and join others who help move this new life along.

I APPROVE OF MYSELF

APRIL 24th

I AM A BELOVED CHILD OF THE UNIVERSE

We all have a purpose. All things are created and grow into what they came here to be, whether it is a newborn puppy or an acorn that becomes a giant oak tree.

JUST FOR TODAY I AM HAPPY AND FULL OF JOY

I came here to be me. I honor all life, tiny and large, because I am aware that everyone matters and deserves to be free.

I APPROVE OF MYSELF

APRIL 25th

I AM A BELOVED CHILD OF THE UNIVERSE

I am free to wonder. My mind is mine to build up, and my imagination belongs to me. I can create, and I can build what I choose and what I see.

JUST FOR TODAY I AM HAPPY AND FULL OF JOY

I am a creator. I can see in my mind what I want to make, and I make it.

I APPROVE OF MYSELF

APRIL 26th

I AM A BELOVED CHILD OF THE UNIVERSE

I can grow things like plants with flowers and even trees with fruit high above. I can take care of living things such as gardens, pets, and the people I love.

JUST FOR TODAY I AM HAPPY AND FULL OF JOY

I can have an idea of how I want my life to be. I plant the seed in my mind, I act, and then suddenly I have created something for all to see.

I APPROVE OF MYSELF

APRIL 27th

I AM A BELOVED CHILD OF THE UNIVERSE

Stillness and calmness come easily to me. I can act after I think about what I am seeing and what I am hearing quite easily.

JUST FOR TODAY I AM HAPPY AND FULL OF JOY

My mind is calm when I want it to be. I have the power to sit still or to move and swish around like the sea.

I APPROVE OF MYSELF

APRIL 28th

I AM A BELOVED CHILD OF THE UNIVERSE

I am part of a much larger plan. I know that I am loved and that I have been sent here to do what I can to make the world a better place.

JUST FOR TODAY I AM HAPPY AND FULL OF JOY

I have a solid foundation for life like an old redwood tree. I have roots that begin with my family.

I APPROVE OF MYSELF

APRIL 29th

I AM A BELOVED CHILD OF THE UNIVERSE

I let my heart be open to love and kindness as I go through this day. Happiness is a choice. I look towards the glorious sky, walk tall and lift my voice.

JUST FOR TODAY I AM HAPPY AND FULL OF JOY

I will begin again and make today bright. Yesterday is past. Tomorrow is not here. I choose to live in this day only, from morning to night.

I APPROVE OF MYSELF

APRIL 30th

I AM A BELOVED CHILD OF THE UNIVERSE

I am good at lots of things when I focus. I am good at reading, writing, and learning my math. I go to school each day with a decision to listen to others and to be on the achievement path.

JUST FOR TODAY I AM HAPPY AND FULL OF JOY

I focus on what is important to make the world a better place. When I do well at school, I do my part to increase the overall environment of harmony and Grace.

I APPROVE OF MYSELF

"Trust the wait. Embrace the uncertainty. Enjoy the beauty of becoming. When nothing is certain, anything is possible."

—Mandy Hale

MAY 1st

I AM A BELOVED CHILD OF THE UNIVERSE

I am a dancer who can twirl and spin. I can dance anytime I get the feeling from within.

JUST FOR TODAY I AM HAPPY AND FULL OF JOY

Rocking and keeping a beat are what I do when I start moving my feet. I am a dancer, so happy and free. I love it when I get to be me.

I APPROVE OF MYSELF

MAY 2nd

I AM A BELOVED CHILD OF THE UNIVERSE

I am a singer. Singing makes me happy inside. I can sing songs that I learn in school, or I can make up my own songs that help me walk home in a musical stride.

JUST FOR TODAY I AM HAPPY AND FULL OF JOY

I hear music in the wind, the water, and in my heart. I just need to listen because it is there from the start.

I APPROVE OF MYSELF

MAY 3rd

I AM A BELOVED CHILD OF THE UNIVERSE

I am a writer. I learn more each day about how to use my mind to create words and stories. I find it easy to create tales of glory.

JUST FOR TODAY I AM HAPPY AND FULL OF JOY

My imagination is powerful. I can think of a story or a poem. I can tell it to my family, or I can write it down. If I need help, I ask others to help me get my writing off the ground.

I APPROVE OF MYSELF

MAY 4th

I AM A BELOVED CHILD OF THE UNIVERSE

I can grow things like flowers and plants. I set up my garden and welcome the ants. All creatures are precious, and anything can grow when given the chance.

JUST FOR TODAY I AM HAPPY AND FULL OF JOY

I care for my plants and other living things. I enjoy nature and all that it brings.

I APPROVE OF MYSELF

MAY 5th

I AM A BELOVED CHILD OF THE UNIVERSE

I am a gardener of friendships, flowers, and fruit. Anything that comes from that which I plant is a gift from the Universe, from flower to root.

JUST FOR TODAY I AM HAPPY AND FULL OF JOY

I am one of Spirit's bright flowers in the garden along with all the others blessed by the sun. I tend carefully to both flowers and friendships. I am kind to everything and everyone.

I APPROVE OF MYSELF

MAY 6th

I AM A BELOVED CHILD OF THE UNIVERSE

Learning takes me to places unknown. Learning is an adventure that brings excitement and joys of my own.

JUST FOR TODAY I AM HAPPY AND FULL OF JOY

There are many ways to learn. Learning makes me happy and smart. I love to learn as it fills up my heart.

I APPROVE OF MYSELF

I AM A BELOVED CHILD OF THE UNIVERSE

I was made to be someone helpful and keep others in mind. I ask others if they need me to help them with cleaning up, meeting new friends or just passing the time.

JUST FOR TODAY I AM HAPPY AND FULL OF JOY

It is easy to be helpful. I take care of myself and get lots of rest in order to be there when we are expecting a guest.

I APPROVE OF MYSELF

I AM A BELOVED CHILD OF THE UNIVERSE

I have a powerful mind. I allow my thoughts to stream. I see the path to meeting my goal and talk to those I love about my dream.

JUST FOR TODAY I AM HAPPY AND FULL OF JOY

It is okay to set goals, as life is more than it seems. Goals always start with my dreams.

I APPROVE OF MYSELF

I AM A BELOVED CHILD OF THE UNIVERSE

I allow myself to have all my emotions: playfulness, sadness, frustration, wonderment, and joy. Feelings are real and can be as deep and as wide as an ocean.

JUST FOR TODAY I AM HAPPY AND FULL OF JOY

I have seen both rain clouds and sunshine separately and together. Like my feelings, there is all kinds of weather and like the weather, everything always clears up and always gets better.

I APPROVE OF MYSELF

MAY 10th

I AM A BELOVED CHILD OF THE UNIVERSE

I am a lover of learning. Learning happens everywhere and all the time. I learn how to read, do math, and I learn from my past mistakes when I keep an open mind.

JUST FOR TODAY I AM HAPPY AND FULL OF JOY

Everyone makes mistakes. We are human beings, so we are constantly learning with opportunities for retakes.

I APPROVE OF MYSELF

MAY 11th

I AM A BELOVED CHILD OF THE UNIVERSE

Mistakes are part of everyone's life. We do not have to be perfect to be okay. Learning from the past is a valuable life lesson which paves the new way.

JUST FOR TODAY I AM HAPPY AND FULL OF JOY

Sometimes I miss the mark. I learn what I did wrong, say I am sorry if needed, and then I simply restart.

I APPROVE OF MYSELF

MAY 12th

I AM A BELOVED CHILD OF THE UNIVERSE

Making an amend to right a wrong is a critical part of how I grow. When I am wrong, I admit it and easily forgive myself, and I forgive others I know.

JUST FOR TODAY I AM HAPPY AND FULL OF JOY

Apologizing is a tool in my toolbox for a successful life. Using it keeps me at peace and living right.

I APPROVE OF MYSELF

MAY 13th

I AM A BELOVED CHILD OF THE UNIVERSE

I am careful to be kind and caring to all I meet. I am calm and listen when I meet someone new. I like to help people feel included in case they feel different from me or from you.

JUST FOR TODAY I AM HAPPY AND FULL OF JOY

Sometimes people feel left out, so I practice including others when I am out and about.

I APPROVE OF MYSELF

MAY 14th

I AM A BELOVED CHILD OF THE UNIVERSE

I find joy in change. Everything is changing in springtime. I feel light hearted playing on the grass and running through the fields with your hand in mine.

JUST FOR TODAY I AM HAPPY AND FULL OF JOY

I have everything I need to learn something new: intelligence, strength, and fearlessness too.

I APPROVE OF MYSELF

MAY 15th

I AM A BELOVED CHILD OF THE UNIVERSE

I finish what I start. When I start a project, I follow it through even when it gets difficult and I want to tear it apart.

JUST FOR TODAY I AM HAPPY AND FULL OF JOY

I am learning how to grow up inside. It is not always easy to finish what I start, and sometimes I would like to set things aside. But I am resilient and steady. I can always take a rest when I need to and come back to finish when I am ready.

I APPROVE OF MYSELF

MAY 16th

I AM A BELOVED CHILD OF THE UNIVERSE

I can grow things and make new life. I can plant a seed in the ground, care for it and watch life come around.

JUST FOR TODAY I AM HAPPY AND FULL OF JOY

I can care for things and support a new start. I cherish all living things, and in making the world better, I always do my small part.

I APPROVE OF MYSELF

MAY 17th

I AM A BELOVED CHILD OF THE UNIVERSE

I encourage others to do their best, whether it is at home cleaning their space or at school on a test.

JUST FOR TODAY I AM HAPPY AND FULL OF JOY

When others are in the middle of a hard lesson, I am here to be a friend. Life is a cooperation and not a competition, so I make sure others feel they are supported to the end.

I APPROVE OF MYSELF

MAY 18th

I AM A BELOVED CHILD OF THE UNIVERSE

I am careful to be quiet while others study or rest. I am considerate while others to do what they need to do to be at their best.

JUST FOR TODAY I AM HAPPY AND FULL OF JOY

I can support others in reaching their goals and dreams. I am not the only one that needs to belong to a team.

I APPROVE OF MYSELF

MAY 19th

I AM A BELOVED CHILD OF THE UNIVERSE

I choose friends who support my best behavior and care about my safety. My friends reflect who I am, so I choose them carefully.

JUST FOR TODAY I AM HAPPY AND FULL OF JOY

Surrounding myself with friends who are kind is my number one goal. Kind people live life from a place that is whole.

I APPROVE OF MYSELF

MAY 20th

I AM A BELOVED CHILD OF THE UNIVERSE

I am confident that my future is bright. I keep moving forward with my goals as my light.

JUST FOR TODAY I AM HAPPY AND FULL OF JOY

I see the glass half full and the river streaming my way. When I hop on the boat flowing easily down the river of life, my work feels like play.

I APPROVE OF MYSELF

MAY 21st

I AM A BELOVED CHILD OF THE UNIVERSE

I am reliable. When I volunteer to do the job, I follow through to the end. Keeping my word is part of being a good family member and a good friend.

JUST FOR TODAY I AM HAPPY AND FULL OF JOY

Keeping my word is important, so I follow through. This makes for a healthy relationship between me and you.

I APPROVE OF MYSELF

MAY 22nd

I AM A BELOVED CHILD OF THE UNIVERSE

I am thorough When I am given a job to do. I ask for help if needed, and I am happy to give help to others too.

JUST FOR TODAY I AM HAPPY AND FULL OF JOY

Finishing my task is rewarding and creates joy in my day. Finishing feels good and means I do what I say.

I APPROVE OF MYSELF

MAY 23rd

I AM A BELOVED CHILD OF THE UNIVERSE

I help others without expecting anything in return. I know that giving something is the same as getting something. The act of giving makes me feel joy.

JUST FOR TODAY I AM HAPPY AND FULL OF JOY

When someone needs something from me, I give with no condition. I get the benefit of a joyful disposition. Giving and getting are the same proposition.

I APPROVE OF MYSELF

MAY 24th

I AM A BELOVED CHILD OF THE UNIVERSE

My job is to grow and learn the best I can. I take in the world with an open mind and give a helping hand. I take care of myself so that when you need me, it is with you that I will stand.

JUST FOR TODAY I AM HAPPY AND FULL OF JOY

I am a good friend. Part of being a good friend is making good decisions that support both myself and others to act from a place of truth and kindness.

I APPROVE OF MYSELF

MAY 25th

I AM A BELOVED CHILD OF THE UNIVERSE

I love to go on adventures. When I see the kite fly higher and higher, my soul feels happy as though it could soar to the wire.

JUST FOR TODAY I AM HAPPY AND FULL OF JOY

Adventures are exciting like flying a kite. When I am out with my family and friends, my heart feels just right.

I APPROVE OF MYSELF

MAY 26th

I AM A BELOVED CHILD OF THE UNIVERSE

Today I am getting ready to learn something new. Each day I am excited by what I can learn and by what I can do.

JUST FOR TODAY I AM HAPPY AND FULL OF JOY

My thoughts are clear, and my choices are many. I am free to make decisions on how to spend both my time and my money.

I APPROVE OF MYSELF

MAY 27th

I AM A BELOVED CHILD OF THE UNIVERSE

I can be a leader, or I can be one of the crowd. I am always careful to use my words and make sure that my actions are proud.

JUST FOR TODAY I AM HAPPY AND FULL OF JOY

Everyone needs positive direction. When asked, I provide guidance to others with love and affection.

APPROVE OF MYSELF

MAY 28th

I AM A BELOVED CHILD OF THE UNIVERSE

I find joy in all living things. I hear the birds singing. I am excited for the brand-new day. I listen to and respect nature as I get on my way.

JUST FOR TODAY I AM HAPPY AND FULL OF JOY

The song of the birds soothes my heart. I plan to have a good day by being a kind person and by doing my part.

I APPROVE OF MYSELF

MAY 29th

I AM A BELOVED CHILD OF THE UNIVERSE

I want to succeed in all that I do. However, I know that it is important that I compromise too.

JUST FOR TODAY I AM HAPPY AND FULL OF JOY

Winning is fun and makes me feel great. I also know that winning is not everything and that life is a give and take. Life is for giving. Living in community is my choice to create.

I APPROVE OF MYSELF

MAY 30th

I AM A BELOVED CHILD OF THE UNIVERSE

Kindness towards others is key. What I do is my choice. How I act is my choice. It all comes down to how I use my words and my voice.

FOR TODAY I AM HAPPY AND FULL OF JOY

There is so much to celebrate in this life. If I could choose anything that I wanted to be, I would not want to be anyone else but me.

I APPROVE OF MYSELF

MAY 31st

I AM A BELOVED CHILD OF THE UNIVERSE

I am brave and strong. I belong to a family and a community that celebrates this life as a dance. I am blessed by so much, and I realize that I am not here by chance.

JUST FOR TODAY I AM HAPPY AND FULL OF JOY

The point of life is to find ways to be useful, cheerful, and have a kind disposition. If I can make another happy, then I have fulfilled my heart's mission.

I APPROVE OF MYSELF

"Live In The Sunshine.

Swim In The Sea.

Drink In The Wild Air."

-Ralph Waldo Emerson

JUNE 1st

I AM A BELOVED CHILD OF THE UNIVERSE

I love how the seasons change and that there are times to rest. I enjoy both the summertime of life and the times when I am at school and I must take a test. Summer really is the best.

JUST FOR TODAY I AM HAPPY AND FULL OF JOY

My heart is filled with the magical season of summer when school is out, and I get to run about. My feet are bare, and my face is bathed in sunshine. Being in summer is Divine.

I APPROVE OF MYSELF

JUNE 2nd

I AM A BELOVED CHILD OF THE UNIVERSE

I love the sunshine on a long summer day. I am grateful for school, but I am also grateful I can make time to play.

JUST FOR TODAY I AM HAPPY AND FULL OF JOY

I call up my friends and make time to see them. Each day of summer is another chance to enjoy the restful warm season.

I APPROVE OF MYSELF

JUNE 3rd

I AM A BELOVED CHILD OF THE UNIVERSE

I take good care of my pets. I feed them and make sure they are healthy and clean. They have bodies just like me that require exercise, water, and sleep.

JUST FOR TODAY I AM HAPPY AND FULL OF JOY

Whether it be a dog, cat, or a fish, I must make their space lovely and put food in the dish.

I APPROVE OF MYSELF

JUNE 4th

I AM A BELOVED CHILD OF THE UNIVERSE

Each day is another chance to be me. I like who I am, and I want to share myself with my friends and family.

JUST FOR TODAY I AM HAPPY AND FULL OF JOY

I have value. I belong to everyone. We are all connected. I share who I am because that makes life one that is celebrated, orchestrated, and appreciated.

I APPROVE OF MYSELF

JUNE 5th

I AM A BELOVED CHILD OF THE UNIVERSE

I am a music maker. I can sing, dance, and play instruments if I try and start. There is no limit to how much music I can make when I follow my heart.

JUST FOR TODAY I AM HAPPY AND FULL OF JOY

I can hear music in the ocean and the windy summer breeze. I also feel the music deep inside of me.

I APPROVE OF MYSELF

JUNE 6th

I AM A BELOVED CHILD OF THE UNIVERSE

I cherish the magic of a long summer walk. I can go barefoot, sleep in and see friends on my block.

JUST FOR TODAY I AM HAPPY AND FULL OF JOY

The summer warmth fills my heart and soul. I am enjoying time off to rest. I am whole

I APPROVE OF MYSELF

JUNE 7th

I AM A BELOVED CHILD OF THE UNIVERSE

Today I am immersed in the sunshine inside and out. The days are long, and all things are bathed in sunlight. The golden rays warm my face, and my heart is filled with delight.

JUST FOR TODAY I AM HAPPY AND FULL OF JOY

Summer remembers me each year and embraces me in a warm blanket of love by wrapping me in its long yellow light. It reminds me that I am love and I am loved. Everything will be alright.

I APPROVE OF MYSELF

JUNE 8th

I AM A BELOVED CHILD OF THE UNIVERSE

Happiness is my birthright. Happiness shows up as sunshine, dancing in the summer breeze and being with my family.

JUST FOR TODAY I AM HAPPY AND FULL OF JOY

When I live in the moment of the day, I can let go of any worries, be creative and just enjoy my play.

I APPROVE OF MYSELF

JUNE 9th

I AM A BELOVED CHILD OF THE UNIVERSE

Summertime is a time for reflection and play. I enjoy long days of sun, dreaming and having fun. I make friends easily, and I take time to draw, make art and write poetry.

JUST FOR TODAY I AM HAPPY AND FULL OF JOY

I make friends easily. I shake a hand, I smile wide, and I am true to myself and how I feel inside.

I APPROVE OF MYSELF

JUNE 10th

I AM A BELOVED CHILD OF THE UNIVERSE

My heart is like a summer day. It is filled with light and kindness. I feel like a butterfly, sparkly, beautiful, and bright.

JUST FOR TODAY I AM HAPPY AND FULL OF JOY

I listen to the heart voice inside that guides me to be thoughtful, patient and kind to everyone I meet whether it is at the park or on the street.

I APPROVE OF MYSELF

JUNE 11th

I AM A BELOVED CHILD OF THE UNIVERSE

I am a healer of all things. To all people love and kindness are the magic that I can bring.

JUST FOR TODAY I AM HAPPY AND FULL OF JOY

I am magical when I use my healing light. Healing, patience, and kindness come naturally to me. I am ready to tackle any problem with a loving alchemy.

I APPROVE OF MYSELF

JUNE 12th

I AM A BELOVED CHILD OF THE UNIVERSE

I am a responsible person. When I have chores for the day, I complete them before I leave to go play. I keep my word, and I do my part because I know that is how we live our best day.

JUST FOR TODAY I AM HAPPY AND FULL OF JOY

I enjoy spending time with my family and friends and time alone. Both being with others and sitting with myself makes me happy and fills my soul.

I APPROVE OF MYSELF

JUNE 13th

I AM A BELOVED CHILD OF THE UNIVERSE

I am intelligent. I am brave, and I like to learn new stuff. True power and strength come from what I feed my brain and knowing that I am enough.

JUST FOR TODAY I AM HAPPY AND FULL OF JOY

I have an open mind, and I like to use my imagination to go to new places and think of great things. I add to the world with my thoughts and all that they bring.

I APPROVE OF MYSELF

JUNE 14th

I AM A BELOVED CHILD OF THE UNIVERSE

Listening and observation is how I learn. I can focus my mind and be still for class time.

JUST FOR TODAY I AM HAPPY AND FULL OF JOY

Summer has camps, classes, and camping for fun. Summer is for a different kind of adventure where I can be outdoors learning new things along with everyone.

I APPROVE OF MYSELF

JUNE 15th

I AM A BELOVED CHILD OF THE UNIVERSE

I see the world as a safe and magical place. I listen to my inner voice and to my family when making a choice about who I let into my life and into my space.

JUST FOR TODAY I AM HAPPY AND FULL OF JOY

I am optimistic. I see the glass as half full. I am hopeful. I know that when life gets tough that I will pull through.

I APPROVE OF MYSELF

JUNE 16th

I AM A BELOVED CHILD OF THE UNIVERSE

I accept who I am. I love who I am. I am me, a human still learning to just be.

JUST FOR TODAY I AM HAPPY AND FULL OF JOY

I do what is right. When I listen to my heart voice, I am shown the correct path and then make the right choice.

I APPROVE OF MYSELF

JUNE 17th

I AM A BELOVED CHILD OF THE UNIVERSE

When I am sad, I know things will get better. All things come and go, slow and fast. That is how I know that this too shall pass.

JUST FOR TODAY I AM HAPPY AND FULL OF JOY

I can lift others and myself over hard times by seeing life as a series of chances to be patient and kind.

I APPROVE OF MYSELF

JUNE 18th

I AM A BELOVED CHILD OF THE UNIVERSE

I am grateful. I appreciate what I have, and I take care of my stuff. I know that I have enough.

JUST FOR TODAY I AM HAPPY AND FULL OF JOY

I do my chores and then I go out and play. I help my family organize my day.

I APPROVE OF MYSELF

JUNE 19th

I AM A BELOVED CHILD OF THE UNIVERSE

I build things. When I create, I feel alive and joyful inside.

JUST FOR TODAY I AM HAPPY AND FULL OF JOY

Inspiration is my inner voice urging me to create and dance. I take every opportunity to take the inspirational chance.

I APPROVE OF MYSELF

JUNE 20th

I AM A BELOVED CHILD OF THE UNIVERSE

I enjoy my family, loving and strong. We may not be perfect but to each other we belong.

JUST FOR TODAY I AM HAPPY AND FULL OF JOY

No matter the weather, sunny, cloudy, or gray, we were meant to be together each day.

I APPROVE OF MYSELF

JUNE 21st

I AM A BELOVED CHILD OF THE UNIVERSE

I can change my mood for the better. When I am feeling low, I can reach out to my family or a friend and tell them I am in need of a lift. When I do this, it is my attitude that will shift.

JUST FOR TODAY I AM HAPPY AND FULL OF JOY

I can start my day over at any time. I just pause for a moment and allow stillness to take over my mind. I remember my blessings and the promise that everything will turn out just fine.

I APPROVE OF MYSELF

JUNE 22nd

I AM A BELOVED CHILD OF THE UNIVERSE

Keeping my word is important to me. I am a trustworthy person for others to see.

JUST FOR TODAY I AM HAPPY AND FULL OF JOY

Healthy relationships are based on our words and actions. I know that to follow through is important to me and to you.

I APPROVE OF MYSELF

JUNE 23rd

I AM A BELOVED CHILD OF THE UNIVERSE

I was born to make the world a better place. I carefully plan with my family on how to exercise this Grace.

JUST FOR TODAY I AM HAPPY AND FULL OF JOY

Although I am a small part, I have so much to give. I do not squander my talent, my time, or the life that I live.

I APPROVE OF MYSELF

JUNE 24th

I AM A BELOVED CHILD OF THE UNIVERSE

Hope springs eternal and my heart is full of hope for all I see. I hope for tomorrow to be better for those who are less fortunate than me.

JUST FOR TODAY I AM HAPPY AND FULL OF JOY

I am compassionate and loving to others in need.

I APPROVE OF MYSELF

JUNE 25th

I AM A BELOVED CHILD OF THE UNIVERSE

It feels good choosing the right thing to do. This allows for a healthy relationship for both me and for you.

JUST FOR TODAY I AM HAPPY AND FULL OF JOY

When I make a mistake, I can forgive myself. When I practice forgiving myself, I can forgive others too.

I APPROVE OF MYSELF

JUNE 26th

I AM A BELOVED CHILD OF THE UNIVERSE

I like to take time in the afternoon to rest quietly in my own space. I am soothed with time on my own and in my quiet place.

JUST FOR TODAY I AM HAPPY AND FULL OF JOY

Thinking my own thoughts in stillness, takes my soul to a place I like to go.

I APPROVE OF MYSELF

JUNE 27th

When I feel sad or even mad, I know I can pause for a moment and think of all of those that I love and of those that love me. This loving energy will help me to stay calm and will open a clear path for me to see.

JUST FOR TODAY I AM HAPPY AND FULL OF JOY

I am surrounded and held by generations of strong, fair, and kind people. I know that the energy that I put out will always come back without a doubt.

I APPROVE OF MYSELF

JUNE 28th

I AM A BELOVED CHILD OF THE UNIVERSE

I throw my trash away in a bin or a can. I look around to see if there is litter on the ground and I throw that away too, in order to keep my community clean and serene.

JUST FOR TODAY I AM HAPPY AND FULL OF JOY

This one world we live in was made for me and you, and everything we do to take care of it will help keep the skies clean and blue.

I APPROVE OF MYSELF

JUNE 29th

I AM A BELOVED CHILD OF THE UNIVERSE

I live life by the golden rule: I treat others the way I want to be treated, and that goes for animals too.

JUST FOR TODAY I AM HAPPY AND FULL OF JOY

I love listening to the birds talk and sing in the early morning day. I leave water for them to drink. I like to help in any way.

I APPROVE OF MYSELF

JUNE 30th

I AM A BELOVED CHILD OF THE UNIVERSE

I watch what I do and listen to what I say because I want everything that comes out of me each day to be kind in some way.

JUST FOR TODAY I AM HAPPY AND FULL OF JOY

Being kind is how I prefer to be. I use my words when I am living in community.

I APPROVE OF MYSELF

DAILY AFFIRMATIONS FOR CHILDREN

"Freedom lies in being bold."

—Robert Frost

JULY 1st

I AM A BELOVED CHILD OF THE UNIVERSE

I practice healthy ways to live because I know that my habits add up to who I am—a person who wants to give and understand.

JUST FOR TODAY I AM HAPPY AND FULL OF JOY

In the morning when I wake, I like to meditate because it makes my soul feel great.

I APPROVE OF MYSELF

JULY 2nd

I AM A BELOVED CHILD OF THE UNIVERSE

When I see something good in someone, I tell them. Complementing others is a nice thing to do, and I know it makes me feel good too.

JUST FOR TODAY I AM HAPPY AND FULL OF JOY

I know I am enough. Everything I need in this life I already possess, and all I must do is my best, and the Universe will do the rest.

I APPROVE OF MYSELF

JULY 3rd

I AM A BELOVED CHILD OF THE UNIVERSE

Everything and everyone in this world have at least one strength. Today I shall look for it and say a prayer of thanks.

JUST FOR TODAY I AM HAPPY AND FULL OF JOY

When I choose to see the beauty in everything around me, I feel happy.

I APPROVE OF MYSELF

JULY 4th

I AM A BELOVED CHILD OF THE UNIVERSE

I know that just because someone else has something, it does not mean I cannot have it too. There is enough of everything for me and for you.

JUST FOR TODAY I AM HAPPY AND FULL OF JOY

Life is a cooperation, not a competition.

I APPROVE OF MYSELF

JULY 5th

I AM A BELOVED CHILD OF THE UNIVERSE

I have the strength and willingness to reach high places, and the way to do this is to lift myself and others up with smiling faces.

JUST FOR TODAY I AM HAPPY AND FULL OF JOY

I am what I think about. What I think about makes up me. I choose to think about being happy, joyous, and free.

I APPROVE OF MYSELF

JULY 6th

I AM A BELOVED CHILD OF THE UNIVERSE

If I fall, I get up. If I fail, I try again. I know that life is about ups and downs and turning hard times around.

JUST FOR TODAY I AM HAPPY AND FULL OF JOY

This too shall pass, I know. Every moment runs into the next and every feeling will come and go.

I APPROVE OF MYSELF

JULY 7th

I AM A BELOVED CHILD OF THE UNIVERSE

I do not judge others because I do not know what they had to go through in this life. Instead, I choose to be nice. This I choose because I have not walked in anyone else's shoes.

JUST FOR TODAY I AM HAPPY AND FULL OF JOY

Whenever I get the chance, I choose to encourage people to do their best and I trust that the Universe will do the rest.

I APPROVE OF MYSELF

JULY 8th

I AM A BELOVED CHILD OF THE UNIVERSE

Everyone has their own special time to shine. I must wait patiently until it is mine.

JUST FOR TODAY I AM HAPPY AND FULL OF JOY

I like to share what I have because that is the kind thing to do. I know what I give will always come back tenfold for me and for you.

I APPROVE OF MYSELF

JULY 9th

I AM A BELOVED CHILD OF THE UNIVERSE

The best things in life are free. Sunny days, big moons, trees, mountains, and streams are all here for you and me.

JUST FOR TODAY I AM HAPPY AND FULL OF JOY

I appreciate nature. I see beauty in the smallest bug and the largest creature.

I APPROVE OF MYSELF

JULY 10th

I AM A BELOVED CHILD OF THE UNIVERSE

Each day is a chance to try new things. I can learn to dance, skate, paint, and sing.

JUST FOR TODAY I AM HAPPY AND FULL OF JOY

Staying curious allows me to learn and grow. I can be a part of something new, or I can become the whole show.

I APPROVE OF MYSELF

JULY 11th

I AM A BELOVED CHILD OF THE UNIVERSE

There are no limitations on the places I can go in life. All I must do is what is right.

JUST FOR TODAY I AM HAPPY AND FULL OF JOY

I embrace the future. I will not waste this day or this night with worry and fright.

I APPROVE OF MYSELF

JULY 12th

I AM A BELOVED CHILD OF THE UNIVERSE

I arrived here with freedom ringing in my heart. Each new day I can make a new start.

JUST FOR TODAY I AM HAPPY AND FULL OF JOY

Strong, brave, and amazing inside and out, I use my gifts to help those in need. I can volunteer to feed the hungry, pick up trash in the park, or sing songs for the elderly.

I APPROVE OF MYSELF

JULY 13th

I AM A BELOVED CHILD OF THE UNIVERSE

I am a helpful person. There are so many ways to participate. I can volunteer at an animal shelter. I can pack groceries for those the less fortunate.

JUST FOR TODAY I AM HAPPY AND FULL OF JOY

Giving to others is a way to fill myself up with love and joy. I can be happy with more than just another new toy.

I APPROVE OF MYSELF

JULY 14th

I AM A BELOVED CHILD OF THE UNIVERSE

I am free in many ways. I am free to make good choices. I am free to use my many voices.

JUST FOR TODAY I AM HAPPY AND FULL OF JOY

All people have a right to be free. I support other people's visions and the way they live their life. Freedom means I let others be.

I APPROVE OF MYSELF

JULY 15th

I AM A BELOVED CHILD OF THE UNIVERSE

I like making plans with my family and friends. We can make an entire day full of adventures and things to do from beginning to end.

JUST FOR TODAY I AM HAPPY AND FULL OF JOY

I am good at planning out things and deciding what I am going to do. My heart and mind feel good when I accomplish something that I have planned to pursue.

I APPROVE OF MYSELF

JULY 16th

I AM A BELOVED CHILD OF THE UNIVERSE

I can feel and embrace what is inside of me. I feel what I feel, and I know what I know. Life is not a contest that must be fast or slow.

JUST FOR TODAY I AM HAPPY AND FULL OF JOY

I deserve love and acceptance and the gift of being understood, and so does everyone else in my neighborhood.

I APPROVE OF MYSELF

JULY 17th

I AM A BELOVED CHILD OF THE UNIVERSE

I think for myself; I take care of myself and I respect myself. I am living free.

JUST FOR TODAY I AM HAPPY AND FULL OF JOY

Freedom rings inside my heart and mind and shines through me.

I APPROVE OF MYSELF

JULY 18th

I AM A BELOVED CHILD OF THE UNIVERSE

I possess the freedom to make a choice. Everyone can use their voice to make a choice. If my choice turns out not so great, no worries, there is always another day and another date.

JUST FOR TODAY I AM HAPPY AND FULL OF JOY

It is in the trying it over and over again that I am the winner. All of us can be a new beginner.

I APPROVE OF MYSELF

JULY 19th

I AM A BELOVED CHILD OF THE UNIVERSE

I am curious and want to understand how everything came to be. In asking, I get answers and then believe what is right for me.

JUST FOR TODAY I AM HAPPY AND FULL OF JOY

I can choose what to believe. I can decide how to be. I can move on the path that is right for me.

I APPROVE OF MYSELF

JULY 20th

I AM A BELOVED CHILD OF THE UNIVERSE

I am a responsible person. I keep my word so that others may depend on me to follow through. Freedom involves keeping my word, so I do what I say, and I say what I do.

JUST FOR TODAY I AM HAPPY AND FULL OF JOY

Picking up the house, weeding the garden, and doing my part are all the ways that I can live with a grateful and full heart.

I APPROVE OF MYSELF

JULY 21st

I AM A BELOVED CHILD OF THE UNIVERSE

I am gracious. I am kind. I love myself and others. I am free to share the love and grace that I have in my life with everyone around me.

JUST FOR TODAY I AM HAPPY AND FULL OF JOY

My life is a beautiful melody of peace and love. My heart feels music deep within my soul, which comes from both inside of me and from the light above.

I APPROVE OF MYSELF

JULY 22nd

I AM A BELOVED CHILD OF THE UNIVERSE

I am loved. I am not alone. Each star in the sky reminds me that I am right at home. I am made up of stardust, and I am connected to all that is good in the Universe.

JUST FOR TODAY I AM HAPPY AND FULL OF JOY

Sharing love and hugging my family makes me feel so good inside. We are all connected and each of us beams with pride.

I APPROVE OF MYSELF

JULY 23rd

I AM A BELOVED CHILD OF THE UNIVERSE

My heart is peaceful because my heart is filled with so much love. I am safe and sound whether I am at home or I am traveling around.

JUST FOR TODAY I AM HAPPY AND FULL OF JOY

Like fireworks, I can become angry and a spark runs through me until it burns out. When I take a deep breath, the spark passes with ease. After this deep breath, I am once again at peace.

I APPROVE OF MYSELF

JULY 24th

I AM A BELOVED CHILD OF THE UNIVERSE

I like a good adventure. I like camping in the mountains or in my own backyard. When I am with my family, nothing feels very hard.

JUST FOR TODAY I AM HAPPY AND FULL OF JOY

Adventure, mystery, and the unknown; there are so many things that await me in books and in real life. So many places to go and see because the world is open to me.

I APPROVE OF MYSELF

JULY 25th

I AM A BELOVED CHILD OF THE UNIVERSE

I dream of faraway lands. I travel when I read books, see movies, or go on an airplane. The world is big, but we are all the same. We are all connected when peace on earth is our aim.

JUST FOR TODAY I AM HAPPY AND FULL OF JOY

World peace is possible. I do my part by being kind and making sure that everyone understands that they are valuable and smart.

I APPROVE OF MYSELF

JULY 26th

I AM A BELOVED CHILD OF THE UNIVERSE

I create my own environment. I oversee the peace in my own life. I lift my thoughts, and suddenly there is no difficulty or strife.

JUST FOR TODAY I AM HAPPY AND FULL OF JOY

I am connected to everyone and everything. When I am happy, I can spread joy in my home, my neighborhood and in my community.

I APPROVE OF MYSELF

JULY 27th

I AM A BELOVED CHILD OF THE UNIVERSE

I can make anything an adventure, even a tire swing on a tree. I use my imagination to soar high above the clouds and to fly like a bird so free.

JUST FOR TODAY I AM HAPPY AND FULL OF JOY

I can do many things that make me feel amazing inside. I live to the fullest each day, and my Spirit soars like the ocean tide.

I APPROVE OF MYSELF

JULY 28th

I AM A BELOVED CHILD OF THE UNIVERSE

I have enough. There is enough in the world for everyone. There are enough toys, books, love, and food. I have enough.

JUST FOR TODAY I AM HAPPY AND FULL OF JOY

I bring to the world my cup. I dip it into the river of life, and I fill it up. My cup is always full and overflowing. I am enough.

I APPROVE OF MYSELF

JULY 29th

I AM A BELOVED CHILD OF THE UNIVERSE

I make good food choices. Fruits and vegetables from the garden make my mind clear and my body strong. When I eat from the garden it is in excellent health that I move along.

JUST FOR TODAY I AM HAPPY AND FULL OF JOY

My body is a finely tuned machine which houses my Spirit. When I take care of my health, I begin to create wealth.

I APPROVE OF MYSELF

JULY 30th

I AM A BELOVED CHILD OF THE UNIVERSE

I am a beloved member of a family who always keeps me safe. I am cherished and I am loved. I am a child of Grace.

JUST FOR TODAY I AM HAPPY AND FULL OF JOY

I am love and this love radiates through my soul and out to others to help them feel whole. We are all connected.

I APPROVE OF MYSELF

JULY 31st

I AM A BELOVED CHILD OF THE UNIVERSE

I celebrate each day. All my joy comes pouring out and my enthusiasm I cannot contain. There is life that awaits me. Each day I get a chance to be my best self again.

JUST FOR TODAY I AM HAPPY AND FULL OF JOY

Today I celebrate me. I am unique and the only version of me. I am a gift to the world. Love and compassion flow from my heart freely.

I APPROVE OF MYSELF

> "...And All At Once Summer Collapsed Into Fall."
>
> —Oscar Wilde

AUGUST 1st

I AM A BELOVED CHILD OF THE UNIVERSE

My mind is clear as the sea. I can sit still and just think about how great life can be. My mind is clear.

JUST FOR TODAY I AM HAPPY AND FULL OF JOY

A mind that is clear as the sea, is a mind that is happy and free.

I APPROVE OF MYSELF

AUGUST 2nd

I AM A BELOVED CHILD OF THE UNIVERSE

I am healthy. My body is strong, and I take good care of myself. I wash my hands before I eat. I exercise my body each day. I get plenty of sleep.

JUST FOR TODAY I AM HAPPY AND FULL OF JOY

My body is mine to keep safe. It is the temple that houses my Spirit, so I am careful to keep it in tip top shape.

I APPROVE OF MYSELF

AUGUST 3rd

I AM A BELOVED CHILD OF THE UNIVERSE

When I have very strong feelings, I stop for a moment and think before I act or speak. All feelings are okay, but I can stop and breathe when I feel angry, mad, or excited. I can step back if I need to so that my breath and my thoughts are united.

JUST FOR TODAY I AM HAPPY AND FULL OF JOY

Before I start to scream and shout, I take a moment and think it out.

I APPROVE OF MYSELF

AUGUST 4th

I AM A BELOVED CHILD OF THE UNIVERSE

I can wait for things I want. I can send letters, save my money, and practice reading and writing. I am patient with myself and others.

JUST FOR TODAY I AM HAPPY AND FULL OF JOY

Sometimes it is hard to wait. But it is the willingness to wait that will open the gate.

I APPROVE OF MYSELF

AUGUST 5th

I AM A BELOVED CHILD OF THE UNIVERSE

I am happy to pass along my things when I no longer need them. I like to recycle my stuff because I always have enough. Others may be in need, so I part with things easily.

JUST FOR TODAY I AM HAPPY AND FULL OF JOY

Everything is temporary like clothes, books, buildings, and shoes. When I have something that I no longer use, I can pass it along for the next person to choose.

I APPROVE OF MYSELF

AUGUST 6th

I AM A BELOVED CHILD OF THE UNIVERSE

I am a good listener. When I am with others, I can listen to what they have to say. Being a good listener is more important than being a good talker. After I listen, I can reflect, and then I can respond.

JUST FOR TODAY I AM HAPPY AND FULL OF JOY

Listening is a skill that needs practice, just like drawing or becoming an actress.

I APPROVE OF MYSELF

AUGUST 7ᵗʰ

I AM A BELOVED CHILD OF THE UNIVERSE

I think clear and kind thoughts throughout the day. I am the maker of the pictures and the words in my mind. I oversee how my life unfolds. My thoughts are the things my life brings to pass.

JUST FOR TODAY I AM HAPPY AND FULL OF JOY

The world is a big place with lots of different voices, but I can make my day happy or sad because I oversee my choices.

I APPROVE OF MYSELF

AUGUST 8ᵗʰ

I AM A BELOVED CHILD OF THE UNIVERSE

I care about how others feel. If someone is sick or hurt, I see if I can help them in person or on the phone. I speak to the person and let them know that they are alone.

JUST FOR TODAY I AM HAPPY AND FULL OF JOY

If you are sick or feeling down, I am here, and I will stick around.

I APPROVE OF MYSELF

AUGUST 9ᵗʰ

I AM A BELOVED CHILD OF THE UNIVERSE

I take care of my things. I make my bed, pick up my toys, and dust off my books. I like to keep my space tidy, and I care how things look.

JUST FOR TODAY I AM HAPPY AND FULL OF JOY

I am considerate of myself and others when I take care of my space. I belong to a family and each of us has our place. A clean place is a happy space.

I APPROVE OF MYSELF

AUGUST 10th

I AM A BELOVED CHILD OF THE UNIVERSE

I am full of ideas and questions. Before I start my day, I can I reach out to the stillness from deep within me and find a place of peace.

JUST FOR TODAY I AM HAPPY AND FULL OF JOY

I see my reflection in the water or a mirror and know who I see. I am open to love and secure in who I am and who I want to be.

I APPROVE OF MYSELF

AUGUST 11th

I AM A BELOVED CHILD OF THE UNIVERSE

I am grateful for everything that I have in my life. I have all that I need. I have a thankful heart. I have everything I need each day to make a new start.

JUST FOR TODAY I AM HAPPY AND FULL OF JOY

A grateful heart never doubts that the world is inherently well and that we are here to help.

I APPROVE OF MYSELF

AUGUST 12th

I AM A BELOVED CHILD OF THE UNIVERSE

I look in the mirror and see the beauty of me.

JUST FOR TODAY I AM HAPPY AND FULL OF JOY

Like a river that moves gently, my heart is filled with love. I let the river of tenderness and compassion fill me up.

I APPROVE OF MYSELF

AUGUST 13th

I AM A BELOVED CHILD OF THE UNIVERSE

I cooperate with others. Getting along is important and respectful. I cooperate with others to promote harmony in my family, at school, and in the park. Cooperation is important to the community.

JUST FOR TODAY I AM HAPPY AND FULL OF JOY

I can share, wait in line, and offer to get the dog leash. These are all the ways that I show my desire to promote peace.

I APPROVE OF MYSELF

AUGUST 14th

I AM A BELOVED CHILD OF THE UNIVERSE

When I have very strong feelings, I stop for a moment and think before I act or speak. I am human, so I have lots of feelings. Feelings run from happy to sad. None of my feelings are bad.

JUST FOR TODAY I AM HAPPY AND FULL OF JOY

I create my own environment. Before I start to shout too loud or use my hands to hit, I take a moment and often just sit. Hitting is never allowed. I use my words to express myself, and I take a time out if I think I need to shout. I choose peace at home, at school and in the community.

I APPROVE OF MYSELF

AUGUST 15th

I AM A BELOVED CHILD OF THE UNIVERSE

I am a full of light. Deep inside I like doing what is right in my actions and in what I say. Sometimes it is hard to choose to take the right path, but my heart voice helps me find my way.

JUST FOR TODAY I AM HAPPY AND FULL OF JOY

Light shines through me, illuminating my Divine soul. I am happy, peaceful, and whole.

I APPROVE OF MYSELF

AUGUST 16th

I AM A BELOVED CHILD OF THE UNIVERSE

I wake up each day to play and to discover and investigate new and exciting things to do.

JUST FOR TODAY I AM HAPPY AND FULL OF JOY

Each day is a brand-new day, filled with choices and so many things to do and say. I think about how to spend my free time after the work is done and the minutes are all mine.

I APPROVE OF MYSELF

AUGUST 17th

I AM A BELOVED CHILD OF THE UNIVERSE

If I look inside, I will feel the special Spirit that resides in me.

JUST FOR TODAY I AM HAPPY AND FULL OF JOY

If I let love shine out and through, I will see the special person that you are too.

I APPROVE OF MYSELF

AUGUST 18th

I AM A BELOVED CHILD OF THE UNIVERSE

I know peace. I am love. I know who I am and who I came here to be. Anytime I help and I am kind, I am doing what it is the Universe had in mind for me.

JUST FOR TODAY I AM HAPPY AND FULL OF JOY

I share the joy and love that I am. Love and compassion are real. Love and compassion are the greatest gifts that I can give that can help others heal.

I APPROVE OF MYSELF

AUGUST 19th

I AM A BELOVED CHILD OF THE UNIVERSE

This world feels large and unfamiliar at times, but my inner compass knows my own heart and my own mind.

JUST FOR TODAY I AM HAPPY AND FULL OF JOY

I have the intelligence and thoughtfulness to always choose what I do, knowing I will choose what is right and pure and true.

I APPROVE OF MYSELF

AUGUST 20th

I AM A BELOVED CHILD OF THE UNIVERSE

Sometimes it is hard to do what is right, but I dig down deep, and I know that I am supported by the Universal Light.

JUST FOR TODAY I AM HAPPY AND FULL OF JOY

I choose love. To understand others, I put myself in their shoes. When I imagine their difficult walk, compassion becomes easier and then I begin to talk.

I APPROVE OF MYSELF

AUGUST 21st

I AM A BELOVED CHILD OF THE UNIVERSE

Friendships are important to me. I like meeting new people, and I take care of the friends that I have by treating them respectfully.

JUST FOR TODAY I AM HAPPY AND FULL OF JOY

When I get back to school, I will see old friends and I will meet new ones. We will talk about everything we did during the summer break. I look forward to seeing school friends again.

I APPROVE OF MYSELF

AUGUST 22nd

I AM A BELOVED CHILD OF THE UNIVERSE

I make wise decisions. Deciding to listen to those who care for me who are older and wiser is a good decision.

JUST FOR TODAY I AM HAPPY AND FULL OF JOY

I choose. I decide. When I need to reflect on what my choice will be, I use the help of other voices who love and support me.

I APPROVE OF MYSELF

AUGUST 23rd

I AM A BELOVED CHILD OF THE UNIVERSE

I love summertime: collecting things, doing projects, swimming at the pool. Lazy days of summer are ending, and I am feeling like a change is due.

JUST FOR TODAY I AM HAPPY AND FULL OF JOY

I love learning. When I think about schoolwork and field trips with my friends, my heart is happy again.

I APPROVE OF MYSELF

AUGUST 24th

I AM A BELOVED CHILD OF THE UNIVERSE

I am full of love, grace, and peace. All these gifts from the Universe fill me up and add up to what you see.

JUST FOR TODAY I AM HAPPY AND FULL OF JOY

Sometimes difficult emotions fill my soul, but then I remember who I am, and my heart is calm and whole.

I APPROVE OF MYSELF

AUGUST 25th

I AM A BELOVED CHILD OF THE UNIVERSE

I feel alive. I feel alive when I am playing, running outside, riding my bike, and when I am reading a good book. I feel alive when I am learning. It is for more knowledge that my heart is yearning.

JUST FOR TODAY I AM HAPPY AND FULL OF JOY

I see the airplane above and wonder how it can fly. There is so much to learn, and I am so grateful that we have a school nearby.

I APPROVE OF MYSELF

AUGUST 26th

I AM A BELOVED CHILD OF THE UNIVERSE

I am going to have a good day. I am not sure how his day will go, or what will happen, but I do know I am going to have a good day because I decide to be open and grateful.

JUST FOR TODAY I AM HAPPY AND FULL OF JOY

All the blessings I have been given fill my heart with joy. I am loved. I am useful.

I APPROVE OF MYSELF

AUGUST 27th

I AM A BELOVED CHILD OF THE UNIVERSE

I am always growing and changing. I embrace all of me during every stage and phase.

JUST FOR TODAY I AM HAPPY AND FULL OF JOY

I am love itself. When I act in any other way, I feel a bit off center. At my core I am a loving and kind person. I may be growing up taller or starting a new year, but my core self remains steady and clear.

I APPROVE OF MYSELF

AUGUST 28th

I AM A BELOVED CHILD OF THE UNIVERSE

I cannot wait to seize this day. The sun is shining, and I am rested, so I will go outside and play.

JUST FOR TODAY I AM HAPPY AND FULL OF JOY

I like reading and discovering new and magical adventures. I have an active imagination, and I use it every day.

I APPROVE OF MYSELF

AUGUST 29th

I AM A BELOVED CHILD OF THE UNIVERSE

I am here for my family to care, to love, to lift them up when they are sad and need a helping hand or someone to understand.

JUST FOR TODAY I AM HAPPY AND FULL OF JOY

I give from my heart all the beauty and love that has been given to me. Love flows through me like a waterfall overflowing.

I APPROVE OF MYSELF

AUGUST 30th

I AM A BELOVED CHILD OF THE UNIVERSE

I have a vision. I may be a writer or a musician or anything else that I choose. I must go to school and do my job of learning to do the things I want to do.

JUST FOR TODAY I AM HAPPY AND FULL OF JOY

Having a dream of what I want to be is just as important as going to school. I have a dream and I want to learn as much as I can acquire. School is a tool to realize the vision of my desire.

I APPROVE OF MYSELF

AUGUST 31ST

I AM A BELOVED CHILD OF THE UNIVERSE

I embrace the future full of surprises and unknown things. I have the strength and the courage to change and grow. When I am brave, I have an inner glow.

JUST FOR TODAY I AM HAPPY AND FULL OF JOY

I am brave, kind, tenderhearted, and true. These attributes run through me and it is who I want to be for me and for you.

I APPROVE OF MYSELF

> "Education is the key to unlocking the world, a passport to freedom."
>
> —Oprah Winfrey

SEPTEMBER 1st

I AM A BELOVED CHILD OF THE UNIVERSE

Getting quiet helps me think. I like to think of all kinds of things. Thinking helps me to use my imagination and embrace all that life brings.

JUST FOR TODAY I AM HAPPY AND FULL OF JOY

Magic can happen when I think. Getting quiet and sitting still to think is my choice today and helps me with what I do and say.

I APPROVE OF MYSELF

SEPTEMBER 2nd

I AM A BELOVED CHILD OF THE UNIVERSE

I choose to wear clothing that is comfortable and clean. I value my body and my health. With others, I set limits on how they can treat me and my body. My mind and body are serene.

JUST FOR TODAY I AM HAPPY AND FULL OF JOY

I know what to wear for school or play, and I show others that I respect myself with the choices that I make each day.

I APPROVE OF MYSELF

SEPTEMBER 3rd

I AM A BELOVED CHILD OF THE UNIVERSE

I like to learn. Learning gives me a sense of power. When I am in class learning new things, it makes me feel smarter by the hour.

JUST FOR TODAY I AM HAPPY AND FULL OF JOY

Writing, singing, reading and math are all setting me on the success path. My job is to learn to be my best. I understand that we all do our part to make the world good for the rest.

I APPROVE OF MYSELF

SEPTEMBER 4th

I AM A BELOVED CHILD OF THE UNIVERSE

Learning makes me powerful. It is my job to learn at school and when I am at play. I study each day to unfold all the knowledge that I came here to display.

JUST FOR TODAY I AM HAPPY AND FULL OF JOY

Whether it is math, reading, or art, practicing new things makes my heart sing.

I APPROVE OF MYSELF

SEPTEMBER 5th

I AM A BELOVED CHILD OF THE UNIVERSE

We are all connected. We come from different places and families, but we are all part of the same human family, and we all want the same things: to belong, to be appreciated, and to be loved.

JUST FOR TODAY I AM HAPPY AND FULL OF JOY

I celebrate our differences, but I also know that we want many of the same things.
I share praise and kindness all around. I tell others how wonderful it is to be with them at school and on the playground.

I APPROVE OF MYSELF

SEPTEMBER 6th

I AM A BELOVED CHILD OF THE UNIVERSE

I am dependable. What I say is what I do, and what I do is what I say. Doing what I say I am going to do is important to show that I can keep my word. I do not make a promise unless I plan to follow through undeterred.

JUST FOR TODAY I AM HAPPY AND FULL OF JOY.

I oversee my actions and my words. If I say that I will help you, then I will do my best to follow through.

I APPROVE OF MYSELF

SEPTEMBER 7th

I AM A BELOVED CHILD OF THE UNIVERSE

I take care of my things. I make my bed, pick up my toys, and take out my garbage. I like to keep my space tidy.

JUST FOR TODAY I AM HAPPY AND FULL OF JOY

I am considerate of myself and others when I take care of my space. I belong to a family and each of us has our place. A clean place is a happy space.

I APPROVE OF MYSELF

SEPTEMBER 8th

I AM A BELOVED CHILD OF THE UNIVERSE

I have control over the thoughts that I think. I can focus and plan my day, then follow through with my goals for work and play. I am the creative and powerful director of my life this day.

JUST FOR TODAY I AM HAPPY AND FULL OF JOY

Whether it is a school day or a day with my family, I control my thoughts just the same. I can make my day interesting and be helpful with my choices that begin with my valuable brain.

I APPROVE OF MYSELF

SEPTEMBER 9th

I AM A BELOVED CHILD OF THE UNIVERSE

I am helpful at home, in class and in my community. I check in with others to see if they need help or even just some company.

JUST FOR TODAY I AM HAPPY AND FULL OF JOY

I am part of a larger community of friends and family. I do my part by sharing my talent, my time, and my brain happily.

I APPROVE OF MYSELF

SEPTEMBER 10th

I AM A BELOVED CHILD OF THE UNIVERSE

I make good choices and doing what is right is naturally a part of me. Sometimes it is hard to know what path to choose, but my heart voice will tell me which way to go.

JUST FOR TODAY I AM HAPPY AND FULL OF JOY

My Creator shines through me, illuminating my way. I sit quiet for a moment. I listen and then I know how to act positively throughout my day.

I APPROVE OF MYSELF

SEPTEMBER 11th

I AM A BELOVED CHILD OF THE UNIVERSE

I clean up after myself at home, at school and in the community. When everyone does their part, the oceans are cleaner and the air we breathe is good for our lungs and our heart.

JUST FOR TODAY I AM HAPPY AND FULL OF JOY

The earth is a living thing like the oceans and the streams. Every bit matters when taking care of the earth, from picking up litter to turning off lights. Caring for our planet is the way to live right.

I APPROVE OF MYSELF

SEPTEMBER 12th

I AM A BELOVED CHILD OF THE UNIVERSE

When I have very strong feelings, I stop for a moment and think before I speak. My heart voice can guide me every time. I remember to pay attention to this inner voice of mine.

JUST FOR TODAY I AM HAPPY AND FULL OF JOY

I am in control of my behavior. I can choose to be kind no matter what others do, to my heart voice I will always be true.

I APPROVE OF MYSELF

SEPTEMBER 13th

I AM A BELOVED CHILD OF THE UNIVERSE

I know that one small seed can grow into a huge redwood tree. I believe that I can make anything come to be. I believe in the unlimited power of Creation.

JUST FOR TODAY I AM HAPPY AND FULL OF JOY

If I think I can, I can. What I think I am, I am. I can dream of what I want to be and what I want to do and do it because I am powerfully me.

I APPROVE OF MYSELF

SEPTEMBER 14th

I AM A BELOVED CHILD OF THE UNIVERSE

I plan. I decide how to spend each day. There are things I must do like going to school, but I can plan to have a productive day and do my best. I decide how to dress, pack my lunch, do my homework, keep my spaces tidy and to study for my test.

JUST FOR TODAY I AM HAPPY AND FULL OF JOY

I am intelligent, thoughtful, and grateful. Planning is good but sometimes plans need to change, if needed I can be flexible.

I APPROVE OF MYSELF

SEPTEMBER 15th

I AM A BELOVED CHILD OF THE UNIVERSE

Today I begin again. I can start something new and finish what I started. Both the new and the old come together to create a life that is wholehearted.

JUST FOR TODAY I AM HAPPY AND FULL OF JOY

My mind and my heart work together, allowing me to oversee myself and to live in this day. I use my time, my thoughts, and my energy to work and to play the wholehearted way.

I APPROVE OF MYSELF

SEPTEMBER 16th

I AM A BELOVED CHILD OF THE UNIVERSE

I love learning new things every day. Knowledge is the way I can empower my dreams to become that which I aspire. Education is the gold that can purchase the life that I desire.

JUST FOR TODAY I AM HAPPY AND FULL OF JOY

How I fill my day shows others I care about myself and my dreams. I realize that how I live is followed by dreams coming true. I live my life with purpose for me and for you.

I APPROVE OF MYSELF

SEPTEMBER 17th

I AM A BELOVED CHILD OF THE UNIVERSE

I look inward where I can see the amazing person inside of me. My thoughts are powerful, my heart voice is wise, and my imagination is as boundless as I want it to be.

JUST FOR TODAY I AM HAPPY AND FULL OF JOY

Today I will live my life like the Source that I am. I will do my best to complete what I start, listen to others, learn something new and give kindness freely to me and to you.

I APPROVE OF MYSELF

SEPTEMBER 18th

I AM A BELOVED CHILD OF THE UNIVERSE

My heart voice was designed to guide me. It came with me at birth. I know what is wrong. I know what is right. Even if others do not agree, I can still trust my heart voice and follow what is right for me.

JUST FOR TODAY I AM HAPPY AND FULL OF JOY

I am not always right with answers at school on a test. However, I am always right when I know what is good for me as compared to the rest.

I APPROVE OF MYSELF

SEPTEMBER 19th

I AM A BELOVED CHILD OF THE UNIVERSE

I have an inner compass that tells me the next right action. If I am confused today on what to do or how to act, I listen to my heart voice. I can trust the words that spring from my heart to make the next right choice.

JUST FOR TODAY I AM HAPPY AND FULL OF JOY

I have the intelligence and thoughtfulness to choose how I walk through this day, on what to do and what to say. I know I will choose what is right, kind, and healthy for me and for you.

I APPROVE OF MYSELF

SEPTEMBER 20th

I AM A BELOVED CHILD OF THE UNIVERSE

I have my own values and my own mind. Other people have their own values and their own mind. We do not always have the same values or make the same choices. It is okay to follow my inner compass, and it is okay for them to follow their inner compass. I do not have to bend my rules to please others. I only must please myself.

JUST FOR TODAY I AM HAPPY AND FULL OF JOY

Compassion is me trying to put myself in your shoes, but it does not mean that I change my thoughts and values. It means that I understand why you choose the way you do.

I APPROVE OF MYSELF

SEPTEMBER 21st

I AM A BELOVED CHILD OF THE UNIVERSE

I make big and small goals so that I have something to work towards. Goals are dreams with a plan and a deadline. I dream of ways to serve the Universe, and I fulfill those dreams in no time.

JUST FOR TODAY I AM HAPPY AND FULL OF JOY

I talk about my dreams. I can write them down or I can draw my vision. Today I am committed to following through with my mission.

I APPROVE OF MYSELF

SEPTEMBER 22nd

I AM A BELOVED CHILD OF THE UNIVERSE

I was created in love by love. I am the vision of my ancestors who imagined me into existence. My natural state is love, kindness and infinite possibility.

JUST FOR TODAY I AM HAPPY AND FULL OF JOY

I decide who I am and what I want to be. I am living my life like those who came before me, a life of kindness and service. Most importantly, I will fulfill my destiny.

I APPROVE OF MYSELF

SEPTEMBER 23rd

I AM A BELOVED CHILD OF THE UNIVERSE

I get an education at school. I get a vision of what I want to be from everything that I learn and see. I use my imagination to create my place in this world to fulfill my destiny.

JUST FOR TODAY I AM HAPPY AND FULL OF JOY

It is never too early or too late to dream and to set myself on the path to success. Once my dream is clear, all that is expected, is that I move forward and do my best.

I APPROVE OF MYSELF

SEPTEMBER 24th

I AM A BELOVED CHILD OF THE UNIVERSE

Love knows no differences. It sees with one lens. The lens of compassion, kindness, and hope for all people on earth. We are one people and we come from one place. We are the human race.

JUST FOR TODAY I AM HAPPY AND FULL OF JOY

I learn from you, and you can learn from me. We belong to one another, no matter who you are, where you are from, or what you have seen.

I APPROVE OF MYSELF

SEPTEMBER 25th

I AM A BELOVED CHILD OF THE UNIVERSE

I am authentically me. I share my thoughts and feelings openly.

JUST FOR TODAY I AM HAPPY AND FULL OF JOY

When I am happy and healthy it is easy to be myself. I stay true to my values, I finish my tasks, I get plenty of sleep and I always do my best. I have good balance between work and rest.

I APPROVE OF MYSELF

SEPTEMBER 26th

I AM A BELOVED CHILD OF THE UNIVERSE

My actions show my character. I am careful to choose my thoughts because thoughts cause action. If I think loving and kind thoughts, my actions will be loving and kind.

JUST FOR TODAY I AM HAPPY AND FULL OF JOY

I want to leave things better than how I found them. I want to leave people glad that we met. I will not forget to speak low and kindly when I meet new friends. I will pick up after myself when I leave a place that I have been.

I APPROVE OF MYSELF

SEPTEMBER 27th

I AM A BELOVED CHILD OF THE UNIVERSE

I can be brave. When I need to be brave, I am strong. When I am getting a shot, speaking in class, or learning to ride my bike, I take courage along.

JUST FOR TODAY I AM HAPPY AND FULL OF JOY

When I take a risk like speaking out loud, it is of myself, that I am so proud.

I APPROVE OF MYSELF

SEPTEMBER 28th

I AM A BELOVED CHILD OF THE UNIVERSE

I have more than I could ever need. My blessings are too many to count. When I see someone that is less fortunate, I want to find a way to help them out.

JUST FOR TODAY I AM HAPPY AND FULL OF JOY

I imagine a world of peace, love, and harmony, and it all starts with me.

I APPROVE OF MYSELF

SEPTEMBER 29th

I AM A BELOVED CHILD OF THE UNIVERSE

If we disagree, we can still talk to each other respectfully. Everyone has their own opinion and that is okay, we do not all have to think the exact same way.

JUST FOR TODAY I AM HAPPY AND FULL OF JOY

A form of love is to listen carefully to another person's point of view. Listening is the loving act. Agreeing with them is a choice but is not as important as taking turns sharing our voice.

I APPROVE OF MYSELF

SEPTEMBER 30th

I AM A BELOVED CHILD OF THE UNIVERSE

Going to school is my job. Having a vision for myself is my gift to the Universe. I use both my education and my vision to achieve my goal.

JUST FOR TODAY I AM HAPPY AND FULL OF JOY

I take time to plan my day. I take time to plan the ways that I can serve the planet so that I can achieve the desires of my soul.

I APPROVE OF MYSELF

"I am my ancestor's wildest dreams.
I am my grandmother's prayers.
I am my grandfather's dreaming."

Ysaye Maria Barnwell
- Sweet Honey in the Rock

OCTOBER 1st

I AM A BELOVED CHILD OF THE UNIVERSE

I honor the changing seasons. There is a time for everything. A time for the new and a time for the old. I am reminded of this when the leaves change, and it starts to get cold.

JUST FOR TODAY I AM HAPPY AND FULL OF JOY

Autumn is here, leaves change to beautiful vibrant colors and the ancestors remind us to be at peace. This is the Universal masterpiece.

I APPROVE OF MYSELF

OCTOBER 2nd

I AM A BELOVED CHILD OF THE UNIVERSE

I am a Spirit of change: changing seasons, changing feelings, changing emotions, and changing dreams.

JUST FOR TODAY I AM HAPPY AND FULL OF JOY

Change is good. Nature shows us that the new leaves of spring turn crisp and brown and fall off the tree onto the ground. Just like a tree, I can see what I want to keep and what I want to let go during this time of seasons circling round.

I APPROVE OF MYSELF

OCTOBER 3rd

I AM A BELOVED CHILD OF THE UNIVERSE

I can feel the fall season. Leaves are swirling and flying all around. I am dancing and swaying to the music of the outdoor nature sound. I am in touch with nature from the sky to the ground.

JUST FOR TODAY I AM HAPPY AND FULL OF JOY

I am a nature lover as it makes me feel whole. While dancing and moving I am supported by the Universe to reach any goal.

I APPROVE OF MYSELF

OCTOBER 4th

I AM A BELOVED CHILD OF THE UNIVERSE

I am thankful for this crisp fall day. I will walk through a path of colorful fallen leaves when I go out to make my way.

JUST FOR TODAY I AM HAPPY AND FULL OF JOY

My path is clear and concise. I follow my heart voice and do the next right thing. I know where I am going and the happiness my life will bring.

I APPROVE OF MYSELF

OCTOBER 5th

I AM A BELOVED CHILD OF THE UNIVERSE

I see my dearest friends and family all around me. I have many people around that care how I do. I am helpful and kind so that they will feel good too.

JUST FOR TODAY I AM HAPPY AND FULL OF JOY

Today we can go for a walk and breathe some crisp fall air. We can play and run around without a care. We were made to be joyful each day and to not despair.

I APPROVE OF MYSELF

OCTOBER 6th

I AM A BELOVED CHILD OF THE UNIVERSE

I am inspired by my elders. October is a month for remembering those who came before me. We celebrate those who have passed and make sure that the good that they gave us will last.

JUST FOR TODAY I AM HAPPY AND FULL OF JOY

Grandparents gave us traditions and other relatives gave us the family in which we are raised. I have respect for the ones that came before me and give them my praise.

I APPROVE OF MYSELF

OCTOBER 7th

I AM A BELOVED CHILD OF THE UNIVERSE

I am strong like an oak tree with leaves of gold and brown. It stands there so beautiful and strong even when the wind tries to blow it down.

JUST FOR TODAY I HAPPY AND FULL OF JOY

I know my soul. I come from a long line of loving and kind people. This is the time of year to honor the ones that have made me possible.

I APPROVE OF MYSELF

OCTOBER 8th

I AM A BELOVED CHILD OF THE UNIVERSE

This season of abundance is full of family, celebrations, parties and so much more to do. I am ready to celebrate with others and to honor those who have done so much for me and for you.

JUST FOR TODAY I AM HAPPY AND FULL OF JOY

I love the fall season when everything is changing for me to see. Like many of the changes in life, they move and inspire me.

I APPROVE OF MYSELF

OCTOBER 9th

I AM A BELOVED CHILD OF THE UNIVERSE

I am abundant like this season of celebration for that which we have worked so hard. I find joy and peace in my family and comfort indoors and in my yard.

JUST FOR TODAY I AM HAPPY AND FULL OF JOY

I can ask to rake the leaves and make huge piles. I can fall and jump into them, and then rake them up and do it all over again. Leaf piles bring big smiles.

I APPROVE OF MYSELF

OCTOBER 10th

I AM A BELOVED CHILD OF THE UNIVERSE

I am in tune with the seasons. The beauty of fall is crisp and clear. I also embrace the changes within me each season, and I have no fear.

JUST FOR TODAY I AM HAPPY AND FULL OF JOY

I am held up by a long line of courageous people who came here before me. I have been gifted with grace, faith, and a noble destiny.

I APPROVE OF MYSELF

OCTOBER 11th

I AM A BELOVED CHILD OF THE UNIVERSE

I am thankful for everything. No gift is too small. I have no worries today because I am part of something much bigger and I see it, especially in the fall.

JUST FOR TODAY I AM HAPPY AND FULL OF JOY

I am thankful for my life this crisp, colorful, cold fall day. I will bundle up, and after my work is done, I will go out and play.

I APPROVE OF MYSELF

OCTOBER 12th

I AM A BELOVED CHILD OF THE UNIVERSE

The season brings me to this place of joy where leaves change, and fall is here. I am grateful for this changing time of year.

JUST FOR TODAY I AM HAPPY AND FULL OF JOY

My heart is full of gratitude. My Spirit is joyful and free as I dance around the autumn leaves happy to just be me.

I APPROVE OF MYSELF

OCTOBER 13th

I AM A BELOVED CHILD OF THE UNIVERSE

I am a power for good, and in my work, I take pride. I listen to my teachers, to those who love me and to my own heart voice deep inside.

JUST FOR TODAY I AM HAPPY AND FULL OF JOY

I belong to a community that cares about all human beings, animals, and the planet. I care for my family, my friends, and all sorts of living things. I take nothing for granted.

I APPROVE OF MYSELF

OCTOBER 14th

I AM A BELOVED CHILD OF THE UNIVERSE

What I think about, I can bring about. When I want to do well on a test, I think about how I plan to study and how I can prepare to do my best.

JUST FOR TODAY I AM HAPPY AND FULL OF JOY

The imagination I have is my tool for success. I see myself winning the game or making the dress. What I dream about I can bring about.

I APPROVE OF MYSELF

OCTOBER 15th

I AM A BELOVED CHILD OF THE UNIVERSE

Today my soul is still. I hear the rustling leaves and feel the crisp autumn breeze on my face. This is the Universe in a spiritual embrace.

JUST FOR TODAY I AM HAPPY AND FULL OF JOY

I can make my day what I like. I begin my journey today in that quiet still place.

I APPROVE OF MYSELF

OCTOBER 16th

I AM A BELOVED CHILD OF THE UNIVERSE

I was born into a world of love and possibilities. I make my life what I want it to be with my mind full of ideas and clarity.

JUST FOR TODAY I AM HAPPY AND FULL OF JOY

There is a miracle ready and waiting for me to see on this crisp fall day. I look with fresh eyes, and I create what it is I want the world to be.

I APPROVE OF MYSELF

OCTOBER 17th

I AM A BELOVED CHILD OF THE UNIVERSE

Today I let my love flow through kind acts and by getting up and ready to go. I get up, I show up, and I am grateful to let kindness be my goal.

JUST FOR TODAY I AM HAPPY AND FULL OF JOY

All people are equal. I come from a long line of helpers and justice seeking people. I will continue to do the same, making peace and fairness my heartfelt aim.

I APPROVE OF MYSELF

OCTOBER 18th

I AM A BELOVED CHILD OF THE UNIVERSE

I continue to live my life in a way that will make those before me proud. I will stand up for what I believe and say hard things out loud.

JUST FOR TODAY I AM HAPPY AND FULL OF JOY

I am magnificent and so are you. My life course has purpose and is directed. We are all the same and we are all connected.

I APPROVE OF MYSELF

OCTOBER 19th

I AM A BELOVED CHILD OF THE UNIVERSE

Justice is love in action at home, at school and in the community. Everyone deserves to be treated fairly. I am honest with each person I meet and look at them squarely.

JUST FOR TODAY I AM HAPPY AND FULL OF JOY

What is lasting in this world is that which I give. I freely give my love, my help, and my ideas to help others happily live.

I APPROVE OF MYSELF

OCTOBER 20th

I AM A BELOVED CHILD OF THE UNIVERSE

There is enough for all of us. The world is not a competition, it is an opportunity to share. I win when you win with any test or classroom recognition.

JUST FOR TODAY I AM HAPPY AND FULL OF JOY

I am rich in love, tenderness, and peace. I am joyful when you are brave, and I can see how hard you try to do your best each day.

I APPROVE OF MYSELF

OCTOBER 21st

I AM A BELOVED CHILD OF THE UNIVERSE

Peace comes from justice and fairness. Each time I support what is fair, I feel good inside of me. I will stand up for what is right. I will make sure others feel heard and seen.

JUST FOR TODAY I AM HAPPY AND FULL OF JOY

Service is love out in the open. I live my life knowing that as I help others, my heart is filled up and my joy is deepened. The key to life is giving. This is the key to joyous living.

I APPROVE OF MYSELF

OCTOBER 22nd

I AM A BELOVED CHILD OF THE UNIVERSE

I can create a just and fair world because I can add to the world my compassionate voice. When I see an unfairness, whether to question what I see, is my personal choice.

JUST FOR TODAY I AM HAPPY AND FULL OF JOY

I can add to the work of peace and fairness with my thoughts and actions. I am a peacemaker when I am kind, responsible, and treat those in my life with love and compassion.

I APPROVE OF MYSELF

OCTOBER 23rd

I AM A BELOVED CHILD OF THE UNIVERSE

I am supported by the generations before me who lived full lives and gave of themselves so that I could be here today. My ancestors are reflected in how I live and what I say.

JUST FOR TODAY I AM HAPPY AND FULL OF JOY

I choose to live with purpose and put my ideas out into the Universe. I am alive. I am part of many who came before me, and my soul contains the greatness of many others.

I APPROVE OF MYSELF

OCTOBER 24th

I AM A BELOVED CHILD OF THE UNIVERSE

I come from loving and kind people. I am here as a part of something much bigger than me, and it is something much greater than me, that I can see.

JUST FOR TODAY I AM HAPPY AND FULL OF JOY

My knowledge of how to create things and how to be kind to all people comes from deep within and is with me all the time.

I APPROVE OF MYSELF

OCTOBER 25th

I AM A BELOVED CHILD OF THE UNIVERSE

I live a life of kindness and of fairness. These two ways of being will last forever and are here to make the world a better place for all of us.

JUST FOR TODAY I AM HAPPY AND FULL OF JOY

My mind is wise and listens quietly to what my heart voice says on how to act and how to be.

I APPROVE OF MYSELF

OCTOBER 26th

I AM A BELOVED CHILD OF THE UNIVERSE

I look in the mirror and like what I see. I am a beautiful person inside and out. I look my best each day, and I act in kindness and love. These two ways of living create the person that is me.

JUST FOR TODAY I AM HAPPY AND FULL OF JOY

We each look different on the outside. Inside we are all seeking to live in the sunshine. We all want to be appreciated and to find a way to love and serve others, during this lifetime.

I APPROVE OF MYSELF

OCTOBER 27th

I AM A BELOVED CHILD OF THE UNIVERSE

I am a compassionate person. I try to understand others while at school and at home. I do this by listening to the heart voice inside of me and acting in a way that promotes harmony.

JUST FOR TODAY I AM HAPPY AND FULL OF JOY

Joy is within my heart and I embrace it today. I rise to engage in life and all it has to offer on this magical autumn day.

I APPROVE OF MYSELF

OCTOBER 28th

I AM A BELOVED CHILD OF THE UNIVERSE

For all to live in joyfulness there is a key; everyone has what they need, and everyone feels they are doing each day what they came here to do and be.

JUST FOR TODAY I AM HAPPY AND FULL OF JOY

I believe in miracles, and my heart does too. I am a miracle, and so are you.

I APPROVE OF MYSELF

OCTOBER 29th

I AM A BELOVED CHILD OF THE UNIVERSE

I can see light even on a cold and foggy day. Light slides between the clouds and the sun will always make a way to be on display.

JUST FOR TODAY I AM HAPPY AND FULL OF JOY

I ask for guidance from those I love when I need help finding my way. My heart voice and my inside light will also guide me throughout the night and the day.

I APPROVE OF MYSELF

OCTOBER 30th

I AM A BELOVED CHILD OF THE UNIVERSE

I am connected to everyone and everything. We are different on the outside, but we are the same on inside. Each one of us is a blessing.

JUST FOR TODAY I AM HAPPY AND FULL OF JOY

People may have different skin, body shapes and hair, but we are all the same and need kindness and care.

I APPROVE OF MYSELF

OCTOBER 31ˢᵗ

I AM A BELOVED CHILD OF THE UNIVERSE

Tonight, is a long night that brings a celebration of magical things. On this night I remember those that came before me and did so much for me and my family. They are still with us in the goodness that life brings.

JUST FOR TODAY I AM HAPPY AND FULL OF JOY

I am at peace, I feel safe, and I have no fear of the unknown. I have my guidance from my inner heart voice and from those who came before me. When I remember this, it always brings me to a place inside of me called home.

I APPROVE OF MYSELF

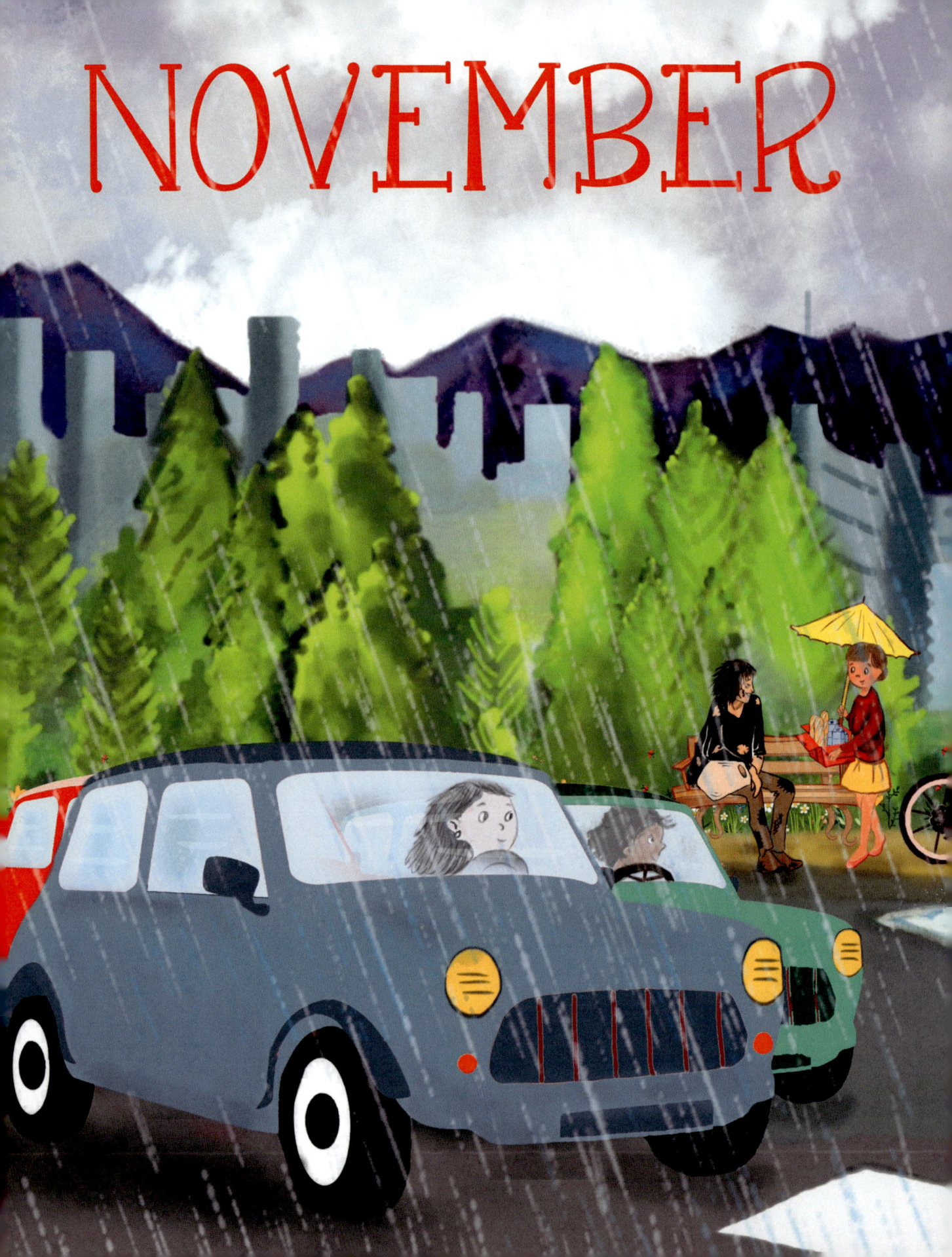

"Gratitude Turns What We Have Into Enough."

—Anonymous

NOVEMBER 1st

I AM A BELOVED CHILD OF THE UNIVERSE

I was born with all that I need to succeed. To succeed I must believe in that which is good. Today I am thankful for every blessing I receive.

JUST FOR TODAY I AM HAPPY AND FULL OF JOY

I have everything I need to be me. I get to build, create, and even imagine the next invention. I bring life to my dreams when I live with intention.

I APPROVE OF MYSELF

NOVEMBER 2nd

I AM A BELOVED CHILD OF THE UNIVERSE

I am love. I am patient. I am kind. I want to share myself with my friends and family and help where I can in my community.

JUST FOR TODAY I AM HAPPY AND FULL OF JOY

I remind myself every day that I am smart, and I am capable. I picture what it is I want to achieve, and out of my thoughts my dreams are shapable.

I APPROVE OF MYSELF

NOVEMBER 3rd

I AM A BELOVED CHILD OF THE UNIVERSE

I am connected to nature and all living things. Nature fills me with a peace that puts my soul at ease.

JUST FOR TODAY I AM HAPPY AND FULL OF JOY

Every morning and every night I take time to remind myself that my actions, words, and thoughts impact everyone and everything around me.

I APPROVE OF MYSELF

NOVEMBER 4th

I AM A BELOVED CHILD OF THE UNIVERSE

Every person has a purpose to fulfill in this world which makes their light shine. I take time to turn inward and listen to the heart voice inside of me that knows the purpose that is mine.

JUST FOR TODAY I AM HAPPY AND FULL OF JOY

When I am brave, I am good at lots of things. When I am creative, I put forth what I came to the world to bring. Using my courage and my imagination makes my heart sing.

I APPROVE OF MYSELF

NOVEMBER 5th

I AM A BELOVED CHILD OF THE UNIVERSE

I can fail with grace. Everyone makes mistakes. I am grateful for each day that gives me another chance to learn and grow which is part of being great.

JUST FOR TODAY I AM HAPPY AND FULL OF JOY

Sharing the lessons that I have learned with others helps the world to heal. I can share what happened and how I made it right. When I apologize, I sleep good at night.

I APPROVE OF MYSELF

NOVEMBER 6th

I AM A BELOVED CHILD OF THE UNIVERSE

I am proud of who I am. I would not want to be anyone but me. I want to help others to believe that they too are just as valuable and unique.

JUST FOR TODAY I AM HAPPY AND FULL OF JOY

I can live a life of service. I help others to know they are valued and have much to give. Everyone matters no matter where they come from or where they live.

I APPROVE OF MYSELF

NOVEMBER 7th

I AM A BELOVED CHILD OF THE UNIVERSE

I have much to be thankful for every second of every day. I will continue to count my blessings whether I am at school, work, or play. For an abundant life, gratitude is the gateway.

JUST FOR TODAY I AM HAPPY AND FULL OF JOY

I want what I have, and I have what I want. Goodness grows inside me each day as I see the good and beauty of those around me. I am thankful for my family, friends, and my community. I have everything I need.

I APPROVE OF MYSELF

NOVEMBER 8th

I AM A BELOVED CHILD OF THE UNIVERSE

There is enough of everything to go around. I am patient when others take their turn whether it is at school, at the park or on the playground.

JUST FOR TODAY I AM HAPPY AND FULL OF JOY

Sharing is love in public. Today I will give something away. It could be a book, a game or something kind that I say. Sharing is kindness on display.

I APPROVE OF MYSELF

NOVEMBER 9th

I AM A BELOVED CHILD OF THE UNIVERSE

I am thankful for the moon and the stars at night. They remind me that everything and everyone was created to shine their own type of light.

JUST FOR TODAY I AM HAPPY AND FULL OF JOY

My light is the love inside of my heart. I know the more I access the power in me, the more the light will grow for others to see.

I APPROVE OF MYSELF

NOVEMBER 10th

I AM A BELOVED CHILD OF THE UNIVERSE

There is beauty in each day. I choose to see the good in others and practice kindness in what I do and what I say.

JUST FOR TODAY I AM HAPPY AND FULL OF JOY

Gratitude and kindness lead me to a place of peace. I am at my best when I say thank you and please.

I APPROVE OF MYSELF

NOVEMBER 11th

I AM A BELOVED CHILD OF THE UNIVERSE

Every moment is a gift. I appreciate what I have right now, and I open my mind to all the possibilities that the Universe will allow.

JUST FOR TODAY I AM HAPPY AND FULL OF JOY

I seize the moment. I cherish the time on this day of mine. I will think of one thing I can do to create an opportunity for me and for you.

I APPROVE OF MYSELF

NOVEMBER 12th

I AM A BELOVED CHILD OF THE UNIVERSE

I have gratitude in my heart from the moment I start my new day. Today I will find ways to give some happiness away.

JUST FOR TODAY I AM HAPPY AND FULL OF JOY

Gratitude is the creator of abundance. I have more than enough of everything, so I am a giver of my time, my energy, my talents, and my guidance.

I APPROVE OF MYSELF

NOVEMBER 13th

I AM A BELOVED CHILD OF THE UNIVERSE

Sharing is love made visible. I share what I have with friends. When someone needs something, I do what I can to give whether it is food, clothing or paper and pens.

JUST FOR TODAY I AM HAPPY AND FULL OF JOY

Today I will find ways to practice sharing with those I meet. I understand that giving and getting are the same energy, which creates more love and abundance for you and for me.

I APPROVE OF MYSELF

NOVEMBER 14th

I AM A BELOVED CHILD OF THE UNIVERSE

What my heart feels is right. I will let that heart voice inside of me be my guiding force in life.

JUST FOR TODAY I AM HAPPY AND FULL OF JOY

Doing the right thing is sometimes hard. Even so, I will be guided by my heart voice in the classroom and in the play yard.

I APPROVE OF MYSELF

NOVEMBER 15th

I AM A BELOVED CHILD OF THE UNIVERSE

I am a spark of the Divine. I possess all that I need to solve problems and to get to the finish line.

JUST FOR TODAY I AM HAPPY AND FULL OF JOY

I cannot control what others say or do. My job is to be my best self and to always show the world who I am even when others are not able to.

I APPROVE OF MYSELF

NOVEMBER 16th

I AM A BELOVED CHILD OF THE UNIVERSE

We are all the same. Each of us has a life purpose that may be different, but on the inside we all want to be our best self at school, home or when playing a game.

JUST FOR TODAY I AM HAPPY AND FULL OF JOY

I know that we have different families, hair, skin, and places to live. That is only the outside. Inside, we all benefit when we find ways to give.

I APPROVE OF MYSELF

NOVEMBER 17th

I AM A BELOVED CHILD OF THE UNIVERSE

Every day is an opportunity to be the best possible version of me that I can be. I use each day to learn and to decide how I am going to serve the Universe. I might be a teacher, a doctor, an artist, or a nurse.

JUST FOR TODAY I AM HAPPY AND FULL OF JOY

Everyone gets to have their life journey and become who they came here to be and do. I do my best to be me, and I am here for others to promote their best selves too.

I APPROVE OF MYSELF

NOVEMBER 18th

I AM A BELOVED CHILD OF THE UNIVERSE

My words have power. I am careful to choose what things I say, so that my words are kind and true each day.

JUST FOR TODAY I AM HAPPY AND FULL OF JOY

I will not forget the promises and commitments that I make. I will try to follow through with what I said throughout the day. Being my word is important to me and to everyone I see.

I APPROVE OF MYSELF

NOVEMBER 19th

I AM A BELOVED CHILD OF THE UNIVERSE

I am compassionate. I will always hold a friend's hand when they are sad or make them laugh when they feel bad.

JUST FOR TODAY I AM HAPPY AND FULL OF JOY

I am the creator of great things like compassion, love, and sincerity. There is an unlimited supply of these ways to improve the world as I move through the Universe as me.

I APPROVE OF MYSELF

NOVEMBER 20th

I AM A BELOVED CHILD OF THE UNIVERSE

Each living person and animal has worth and excellence. I am special and unique, and so are you. I will live my life with compassion and kindness as my world view.

JUST FOR TODAY I AM HAPPY AND FULL OF JOY

I will listen as others speak. I will hear what others say, and I will honor what others contribute to this day.

I APPROVE OF MYSELF

NOVEMBER 21st

I AM A BELOVED CHILD OF THE UNIVERSE

Each person was born to bring their magic to the world. We are all here to love one another and to serve one another. Service is love in action to help my sister or my brother.

JUST FOR TODAY I AM HAPPY AND FULL OF JOY

I have special gifts and talents, and so do you. Everyone has a job to do.

I APPROVE OF MYSELF

NOVEMBER 22nd

I AM A BELOVED CHILD OF THE UNIVERSE

What I choose to think will determine what I feel. What I choose to eat will determine the level of my body's energy and will impact my brain's ability.

JUST FOR TODAY I AM HAPPY AND FULL OF JOY

Today I choose to feed my mind kind thoughts. I choose foods that help my brain think, which allows me to feel happy, joyous, and free so that I can be the best possible version of me.

I APPROVE OF MYSELF

NOVEMBER 23rd

I AM A BELOVED CHILD OF THE UNIVERSE

I am from a long line of people who were brave and worked hard for their families. I have all the best qualities of those who came before me. I am a blessing in a long line of blessings.

JUST FOR TODAY I AM HAPPY AND FULL OF JOY

I embrace my family history. Every family has struggles which helps me learn lessons to stay steady on the beam. I can call on my ancestors at any time to help guide me through life and to keep living out their dream.

I APPROVE OF MYSELF

NOVEMBER 24th

I AM A BELOVED CHILD OF THE UNIVERSE

Today is the only day I have right now to take flight. I will live this day full of gratitude and know that today lived in gratitude will make every tomorrow bright.

JUST FOR TODAY I AM HAPPY AND FULL OF JOY

Today I will find a way to play my part in this great place called life. I know that as I give to the world, the world gives to me. Giving and getting are the same energy and makes my life full and happy.

I APPROVE OF MYSELF

NOVEMBER 25th

I AM A BELOVED CHILD OF THE UNIVERSE

I am a healer of pain and tears with the words that I say. I will choose each word carefully and be sure to say them in a loving way.

JUST FOR TODAY I AM HAPPY AND FULL OF JOY

"I love you" are three little words that can make a big difference in changing someone's attitude and mood, so I will choose to say them to a friend that is feeling blue.

I APPROVE OF MYSELF

NOVEMBER 26th

I AM A BELOVED CHILD OF THE UNIVERSE

I choose how I act even when I get sad or mad. It is important to take a minute to think before I speak. Good and bad feelings are perfectly okay, it is what I do with them that can make or break the day.

JUST FOR TODAY I AM HAPPY AND FULL OF JOY

Today I choose patience and peace with others and with myself. I choose to try to understand what others' think and do and to be okay when I need a hug too.

I APPROVE OF MYSELF

NOVEMBER 27th

I AM A BELOVED CHILD OF THE UNIVERSE

I live an abundant life. I know that there is always more of everything that I need. I have more than enough to share because that is how you show that you care.

JUST FOR TODAY I AM HAPPY AND FULL OF JOY

Caring for others creates abundance. I am blessed to have what I need, and most importantly to know that sharing creates more love, happiness, and prosperity.

I APPROVE OF MYSELF

NOVEMBER 28th

I AM A BELOVED CHILD OF THE UNIVERSE

Every day is another chance to learn and grow. I love reading, problem solving, numbers and playing with friends that I know.

JUST FOR TODAY I AM HAPPY AND FULL OF JOY

What I learn today, I choose to teach. I am willing to share information and the ways that I have solved problems to help others live. All that I have, I freely give.

I APPROVE OF MYSELF

NOVEMBER 29th

I AM A BELOVED CHILD OF THE UNIVERSE

I am playful. I like to dance, play music, draw, and sing. It is important to work, but it is just as important to do what makes me feel light and at ease.

JUST FOR TODAY I AM HAPPY AND FULL OF JOY

I will create beauty with art today. Art is nourishment for the Spirit and is just as important as math, writing and cleaning up my space. In every soul, art has a place.

I APPROVE OF MYSELF

NOVEMBER 30th

I AM A BELOVED CHILD OF THE UNIVERSE

Life is for giving. When I feel like someone has done something wrong, I easily forgive them and then I move along.

JUST FOR TODAY I AM HAPPY AND FULL OF JOY

I can get over it when my feelings are hurt. People are human and make mistakes. I can let it go and start over. I have the power to move on and give people a break.

I APPROVE OF MYSELF

"For each child that is born a morning star rises and sings to the Universe who we are."

– Ysaye Maris Barnwell,
Sweet Honey in the Rock

DECEMBER 1st

I AM A BELOVED CHILD OF THE UNIVERSE

Every child born is the Wonder Child. Every child contains the seeds of hope that can change the world. Every child born brings their unique healing powers to cure what ails us.

JUST FOR TODAY I AM HAPPY AND FULL OF JOY

I am the Wonder Child that was born of love. I am free to choose how I live and how I work on what I came here to do, to help others rise above.

I APPROVE OF MYSELF

DECEMBER 2nd

I AM A BELOVED CHILD OF THE UNIVERSE

Each person is born with their own special healing message to deliver from the start. I listen to my heart voice inside to remind me what I came here to impart.

JUST FOR TODAY I AM HAPPY AND FULL OF JOY

My Spirit is filled with joy and excitement about what today will bring. It is a glorious song that my life will sing.

I APPROVE OF MYSELF

DECEMBER 3rd

I AM A BELOVED CHILD OF THE UNIVERSE

I am a shining star. I am good at many things, like writing, drawing, dancing, and thinking. I am the best version of me.

JUST FOR TODAY I AM HAPPY AND FULL OF JOY

We are all as bright as a shining star. Each one of us has the power to go far.

I APPROVE OF MYSELF

DECEMBER 4th

I AM A BELOVED CHILD OF THE UNIVERSE

I enjoy doing my best. When I take on a job, I put 100% of myself into it. I am happy to do my best cleaning my room or taking a test.

JUST FOR TODAY I AM HAPPY AND FULL OF JOY

What is expected is my best try. I do my best and then I can look at myself in the eye.

I APPROVE OF MYSELF

DECEMBER 5th

I AM A BELOVED CHILD OF THE UNIVERSE

I am the only me on this planet. I am a miracle that shines a bright Spirit that allows me to create peace around me and everyone that I meet on this glorious day.

JUST FOR TODAY I AM HAPPY AND FULL OF JOY

I am a miraculous being filled with wonderment, and a joyful soul. I smile and embrace my good fortune. I am whole.

I APPROVE OF MYSELF

DECEMBER 6th

I AM A BELOVED CHILD OF THE UNIVERSE

I am the wisdom from my ancestor's past. I can see what is pure and true and that which will last.

JUST FOR TODAY I AM HAPPY AND FULL OF JOY

My Spirit came here with a plan. I sit still and listen to my heart voice that is guided by all that I am.

I APPROVE OF MYSELF

DECEMBER 7th

I AM A BELOVED CHILD OF THE UNIVERSE

Love is healing medicine for all that needs to get better. I can extend my heart to help, and we can solve the problem together.

JUST FOR TODAY I AM HAPPY AND FULL OF JOY

Just being open and joyful can help the planet heal. Love can help because love is real.

I APPROVE OF MYSELF

DECEMBER 8th

I AM A BELOVED CHILD OF THE UNIVERSE

I am a gift to this world. I am a healer while at work or at play on this magical, joyful winter day.

JUST FOR TODAY I AM HAPPY AND FULL OF JOY

Holidays are for family and friends to celebrate all that is great. My heart soars high as we plan our time together on our special dates.

I APPROVE OF MYSELF

DECEMBER 9th

I AM A BELOVED CHILD OF THE UNIVERSE

Gratitude fills my soul, a desire to give fills my heart, and being together makes me feel whole.

JUST FOR TODAY I AM HAPPY AND FULL OF JOY

Giving is the same as getting in all things and in all ways. It is the energy of sharing that is the sign of kindness and caring during these celebratory days.

I APPROVE OF MYSELF

DECEMBER 10th

I AM A BELOVED CHILD OF THE UNIVERSE

I count my blessings. I can recite all that is good and right in my life. When I count my blessings, I can see that I am held by the Universal light.

JUST FOR TODAY I AM HAPPY AND FULL OF JOY

Celebrations this month with my family and friends, centers on sharing our blessings and thanking the Universe for what is going well at each day's end.

I APPROVE OF MYSELF

DECEMBER 11th

I AM A BELOVED CHILD OF THE UNIVERSE

I am gifted with the ability to problem-solve. When things get hard, I can also ask for help from those I love. I am not alone, without a doubt. I can count on those around me to work things out.

JUST FOR TODAY I AM HAPPY AND FULL OF JOY

A big part of solving problems is asking for help. My family can help, teachers can help, and others I love are a good choice. To get help, I must use my voice.

I APPROVE OF MYSELF

DECEMBER 12th

I AM A BELOVED CHILD OF THE UNIVERSE

I love being with people I care about during these holiday seasons. Being together makes me happy for so many reasons.

JUST FOR TODAY I AM HAPPY AND FULL OF JOY

Singing holiday songs on a cold winter night makes this magical season so sparkly and bright.

I APPROVE OF MYSELF

DECEMBER 13th

I AM A BELOVED CHILD OF THE UNIVERSE.

I am a creative person. I think of something to create, and I make it happen. This is a magical time of year for baking, painting, making jewelry, drawing, and telling stories about our blessings.

JUST FOR TODAY I AM HAPPY AND FULL OF JOY

I am willing to share my many gifts with others. Giving and getting are the same loving energy. My heart fills up when I give to my sisters and brothers.

I APPROVE OF MYSELF

DECEMBER 14th

I AM A BELOVED CHILD OF THE UNIVERSE

Each child that is born has the power to do great things. I recognize the greatness in everyone I meet, and I bring to everyone my own special being.

JUST FOR TODAY I AM HAPPY AND FULL OF JOY

I embrace the Universal truth that you are a spark of the Divine and so am I.

I APPROVE OF MYSELF

DECEMBER 15th

I AM A BELOVED CHILD OF THE UNIVERSE

My light shines so that others can see that who they are is as magnificent as me.

JUST FOR TODAY I AM HAPPY AND FULL OF JOY

We are on the planet to make a difference while we are here. We are all connected to the Universal plan to share love, kindness, and hope which, once done, will never disappear.

I APPROVE OF MYSELF

DECEMBER 16th

I AM A BELOVED CHILD OF THE UNIVERSE

Today I am my best self. I am a creator of love and healing with my kindness and my being.

JUST FOR TODAY I AM HAPPY AND FULL OF JOY

My life generates peace and harmony. I work each day to be part of the solution, and I try to treat each soul carefully. Everyone has a story.

I APPROVE OF MYSELF

DECEMBER 17th

I AM A BELOVED CHILD OF THE UNIVERSE

This world is a sacred place filled with beautiful places and beings. I respect all living things.

JUST FOR TODAY I AM HAPPY AND FULL OF JOY

I am full of light, beauty, love, and grace. I know who I belong to and where I come from, which helps me to know who I am and how to live in this wonderous space.

I APPROVE OF MYSELF

DECEMBER 18th

I AM A BELOVED CHILD OF THE UNIVERSE

I am full of grace and light. I am human, but I am also a Spirit in flight.

JUST FOR TODAY I AM HAPPY AND FULL OF JOY

Inside I have ideas, feelings, fears, and desires. I am an ordinary person, but I have extraordinary power to use my mind to create beauty, healing, and peace. Everything that was ever created on the earth started with a belief.

I APPROVE OF MYSELF

DECEMBER 19th

I AM A BELOVED CHILD OF THE UNIVERSE

My heart is filled with love and peace during these sacred days, and I am ready to give my time and energy to be with those that I belong, to bake a cake or to sing a song.

JUST FOR TODAY I AM HAPPY AND FULL OF JOY

The seasons of celebration bring me closer to those I love. I count my blessings and honor those that are here and those that have already passed over and are watching from above.

I APPROVE OF MYSELF

DECEMBER 20th

I AM A BELOVED CHILD OF THE UNIVERSE

I was born a sacred and whole Spirit who came here to deliver more love to the Universe.

JUST FOR TODAY I AM HAPPY AND FULL OF JOY

During these long nights and these winter celebrations, I remember that I am here to shine my light brighter than ever across the nation so blessed. I can shine my light by singing, practicing kindness, smiling, spending time with those I love and by seeing others as trying their best.

I APPROVE OF MYSELF

DECEMBER 21st

I AM A BELOVED CHILD OF THE UNIVERSE

I came here to shine my light strong. I have a job to do that makes the world a better place for everyone, even for those who do not think they belong.

JUST FOR TODAY I AM HAPPY AND FULL OF JOY

I am a spark of the Divine and so are you. We are all here with a special job to do. That job is to make the Universe more loving, more kind and more welcome for me and for you.

I APPROVE OF MYSELF

DECEMBER 22nd

I AM A BELOVED CHILD OF THE UNIVERSE

I can see the good in others. I can see when someone is hurt and just needs a hug. I can also see when someone is mad and just needs some kindness. I can see the good in other people no matter what they do. This truth makes the world a better place for me and for you.

JUST FOR TODAY I AM HAPPY AND FULL OF JOY

I am love. Love understands, love is patient and love is kind. During this season of gift giving and gatherings it is important to remember that the best gifts are the ones from the Divine.

I APPROVE OF MYSELF

DECEMBER 23rd

I AM A BELOVED CHILD OF THE UNIVERSE

My life is filled with the wonderment of love and sparkling light.

JUST FOR TODAY I AM HAPPY AND FULL OF JOY.

My Creator flows through me to help me be my best self. I reach out to others who are in need and share this truth. I am love itself and so are you; once we understand this fact, we create goodness in all that we do.

I APPROVE OF MYSELF

DECEMBER 24th

I AM A BELOVED CHILD OF THE UNIVERSE

I am the Wonder Child and so are you. Each of us born from love into this magical place called earth where anything is possible. I seek each day to live my purpose, to love and serve earth's people.

JUST FOR TODAY I AM HAPPY AND FULL OF JOY

How I complete my mission to love and serve on the planet is up to me. I can be and do anything that I can imagine, so long as it is motivated by kindness, compassion, and serenity.

I APPROVE OF MYSELF

DECEMBER 25th

I AM A BELOVED CHILD OF THE UNIVERSE

This is the season of giving, loving, and caring. I am love embodied. I act in love by being present with those I call family and by sharing.

JUST FOR TODAY I AM HAPPY AND FULL OF JOY

Seasons come and seasons go, but my favorite are the winter celebrations of love and the counting of our blessings.

I APPROVE OF MYSELF

DECEMBER 26th

I AM A BELOVED CHILD OF THE UNIVERSE

I do not have to solve problems on my own. Everyone has problems. I share my worries with my family, and I will see that I am not alone.

JUST FOR TODAY I AM HAPPY AND FULL OF JOY

During the winter seasons and all year long, my loved ones are here for me. I share my thoughts and worries, and they can help me be at peace.

I APPROVE OF MYSELF

DECEMBER 27th

I AM A BELOVED CHILD OF THE UNIVERSE

I cooperate with others. Getting along is important and respectful. I cooperate with others to promote harmony in my family, at school and in the park. Cooperation is important to the community.

JUST FOR TODAY I AM HAPPY AND FULL OF JOY

I am an excellent helper. When I notice someone who needs a helping hand, I am happy to follow their command.

I APPROVE OF MYSELF

DECEMBER 28th

I AM A BELOVED CHILD OF THE UNIVERSE

My mind belongs to me. I can have a hard day and still know that my thoughts can keep me peaceful and steady.

JUST FOR TODAY I AM HAPPY AND FULL OF JOY

No matter what is happening around me in the world, I have the power to be still and to know that I am safe. For all things peaceful, I am ready.

I APPROVE OF MYSELF

DECEMBER 29th

I AM A BELOVED CHILD OF THE UNIVERSE

I believe in goodness, love, and kindness. These things make up the best of all of us. We are all connected. Therefore, how I behave impacts how others feel. My actions matter because others are sometimes affected.

JUST FOR TODAY I AM HAPPY AND FULL OF JOY

I impact others with my words, thoughts, and deeds. I am careful to keep a positive and loving attitude with everyone that I meet.

I APPROVE OF MYSELF

DECEMBER 30th

I AM A BELOVED CHILD OF THE UNIVERSE

I am a spark of the Divine. I am unique and different than you. You are a spark of the Divine too. I belong to the Universe, and I create what it is that I was born to create. I am me and I am made up of my own unique recipe.

JUST FOR TODAY I AM HAPPY AND FULL OF JOY

We are One. We are interconnected by love, family, and grace. I have my job and you have yours. All together, we make the world a better place.

I APPROVE OF MYSELF

DECEMBER 31ST

I AM A BELOVED CHILD OF THE UNIVERSE

Every day of the year I have the courage to do what is right. I do the right thing even when it is hard. I am kind and loving to myself and others as a foundation. I move forward in peace and reconciliation.

JUST FOR TODAY I AM HAPPY AND FULL OF JOY

Each new day is a chance to practice being my best self. Being brave does not mean I am not scared, it is feeling afraid, and doing that hard thing anyway for me and for you. Today I let go of the old and I embrace the new.

I APPROVE OF MYSELF

I was Created
I Create
I am a Creator

Made in the USA
Las Vegas, NV
26 January 2021